Wonder, Lost and Found

Books by Hugh Rogers

Beyond Two Rivers
Wonder, Lost and Found

Wonder, Lost and Found

Hugh Rogers

Independently published

Print layout, e–book conversion,
and cover design by DLD Books
Editing and Self–Publishing Services

DLD Books
www.dldbooks.com

Cover image by Hugh Rogers

ISBN: 978-1-7345963-3-5

"Attention is the beginning of devotion."

Mary Oliver

For Monique, Graham and Kelsey

Note

The cover shows the meadow described in the essay "The Ghosts of Peaches" before its destruction. Under permits to qualify for "farm" status and reduced property taxes, the trees were removed, the soil bulldozed, screened, and seeded to lawn.

Contents

Part One
The World at Large

The Last Coal Fire

March 1997

As I was pouring the scuttle of coal this morning before breakfast, I knew it would be our last. There is just no more to be scraped from the bin, only black dust. Not just the last just for this winter but maybe forever, for me anyway, if you can say such a thing. We'll be moving to another house in a month, a house with a more modern heating system, with cast-iron radiators and an oil-fired boiler.

Since the week after Thanksgiving we've carried scuttles of coal from the basement to feed the penguin-sized coal stove in our living room. And we've carried away the ashes, two metal garbage cans a week, to the landfill, where we are told to dump them into the container for building refuse.

Three and a half tons of coal each year, usually three or four scuttles a day, have been converted to heat and ash. I imagine the more than 35 tons of coal burned over the years in one large heap, and I conjure a pile perhaps as large as a two-car garage. Thirty-five tons of anything seems like a lot, especially when you're shoveling it and carrying it upstairs. I won't miss the routine, even though it's been part of winter life here for 11 years. But I will miss the heat, which, with its nearly inextinguishable glow, warmed most of the house and kept the oil furnace silent.

Our boys cover their ears when I pour coal into the stove; it rattles that loudly. And then it crackles like a hundred sparklers on Independence Day. But there was a louder sound, a sound so loud even I had to cover my ears against it. It was the banging of the coal as it ran down the chute off the truck into our bin. A thousand hammers on sheet metal at once. I wondered how the men who delivered the coal could still hear. The truck held ten tons, three separate deliveries. The men would drive all night from the coalfields in Pennsylvania and arrive early, sometimes even in the predawn darkness. More than a few times I was awakened by their arrival and kept them company with a coat over my pajamas.

They were a father and grandson team. The older would talk with us as the younger did most of the heavy work. Although his face held the lines you'd expect for a grandfather, his visage was peaceful. It was the countenance of a man who struggled with no internal stress, a man who was at home with his life and what it had brought him. His eyes twinkled like a coal fire from the youth in his heart.

"Would you believe it? I'll be seventy-seven years old next week and been married to the same woman for fifty years. That's good coal!" he'd shout, watching the black stream flow down the chute.

The first time they delivered, he was in the middle of a sentence when he grabbed a chunk of the black fuel and took my wife's arm in his hand, rubbing her white sweater with the coal. "Look how hard it is!" he yelled. "The next step is diamonds! That's good coal!" We stood, mouths agape, as her sweater was left pure white.

You could tell he knew he was entertaining us, and we were glad he did. It was heartening to see someone so proud of his work, so satisfied with the results of his labor and unashamed of proclaiming it. He knew the people who mined this coal and their histories. He knew where it came from and had lived nearby the mines. In delivering it, he and his grandson were taking forays into the outside world with the coin of their realm and putting it and themselves up as symbols of their homeland and its people, their people. They were ambassadors from the mining country.

They served well, and we will miss them.

A Hole Is to Dig

August 2000

Why do boys dig holes? Why do they build forts? Is it prompted by a dawning awareness that they will someday leave home and they want to practice making a home of their own before then? Are their constructions fortifications against what they know awaits them in the big world out there? Where does this urge to build something come from?

I was out weeding the garden and ended up working near a large hole my sons had dug nearby. It's about four feet across and about that deep. It's quite an excavation for a twelve- and an eleven-year-old, even working together, another aspect of it that struck me. While they were digging it, they cooperated in a way I see them do only when they're inventing a game. They planned, discussed ideas, and took turns down in the bottom and, once the hole became too deep for them to simply shovel the soil out, each would take turns hauling it out with a bucket and a rope. But they didn't stop there. What they next devised, and made from branches and twine, was a tripod from which they hung a pulley. They ran the rope through the pulley and reduced their work hauling the bucket from the hole.

They spent many hours out there, often working until after dark, and were surprised and rewarded when they reached a new layer of soil or had removed a large rock. The challenges the labor provided kept them interested, and the anticipation kept them going. Their excited voices reached my wife and me inside, where we sometimes eavesdropped on their simple joy. And when they had finished that session's work, they were proud to show us what they had accomplished, how far they had come, excitedly telling us of the obstacles they had encountered and how they had overcome them. They were genuinely proud.

Our sons have built different forts, with different materials and under different conditions. Hole forts are just one type of fort, although because they're below ground they perhaps represent the most secure place to build. Last spring they built a large lean-to out of sight of the house, having started with one close to the house first. Their tree forts have gotten higher in the branches, and their means of getting to them has become correspondingly more complex. Their first tree fort was a platform on a hillside they could step onto from the uphill side. Their most recent one involves a rope ladder they pull up after themselves to keep marauders at bay and a pulley to bring up supplies. In the fall, they've made leaf forts, complete with tunnels and chambers of all sizes. Snow becomes the medium in the winter, when they stay out for hours in numbing cold to burrow and build. On rainy days, they've even built forts in the living room with furniture.

For a boy, digging a hole provides a real-life proving "ground" against which he can test himself. With simple equipment and, just as important, no adult supervision, he can safely place himself in an arena full of challenges and create something in his hole or fort that stands for who he is and how he handles problem-solving. It is also concrete. He can see progress, or lack of it, and has something to show for his efforts. He can point to it, touch it, and say, "We made this. Pretty good, isn't it?"

Because it's a project of his own choice, he has a good chance of succeeding. He makes something with his bare hands and his imagination from just the raw materials he's found in his environment. He did it on his own, and the self-reliance has tested not only his creativity but his tenacity as well. It takes an undefeatable spirit to keep going despite problems. He is inspired by challenges—"How deep can we make it?" He also begins to understand what commitment to a goal means and begins to appreciate what hard work in pursuit of that goal entails.

Often, these projects are cooperative in nature. In fact, now that I think of it, I don't ever remember building a fort or digging a hole by myself. Boys learn that the exchange of ideas in a respectful fashion is necessary, as a fight will end the fun they themselves have created and are having. They learn about division of labor ("You dig and I'll haul") and equal contribution ("My turn to dig"). Along with this comes recognition and respect for different levels of task difficulty and about matching tasks with strengths ("You're taller, so you place the high branches; I'll collect the sticks").

They have a companion on this metaphorical project and learn they are not alone. And from that they learn compassion. ("We need to help each other out.")

Along the way, a boy learns about craftsmanship. ("We'd better dig this part out now or it might collapse later.")

But perhaps the simple answer to the question of why boys do this is curiosity. ("What's down there? How far can we go?") Children have a natural capacity for wonder, and beginning with the earth under your feet is organic to their thinking.

We have become an information rich and experience poor society, and as the distance between us and our natural world increases, I like to think there are boys out there who are still digging holes, building forts, and absorbing the wealth of their endeavors. I am tempted, the next time I interview a male candidate for a teaching job at my school to begin, not with the standard educational queries, but with: "Tell me about the forts you built when you were a kid." I'm convinced I'd get a fair measure, not only of his competence but also of his imagination.

An Open Letter to Henry Thoreau

November 2002

I've just finished reading a play about you, Henry, called *The Night Thoreau Spent in Jail*, and was struck by how strongly you stood for principles carried to their logical conclusion. You refused to support your government's war on Mexico (it was an unjust taking of their land), and, because of this, you refused to pay your taxes or let anyone pay them for you.

How many of us would do the same? I do not support the "war" on terrorism that limits our freedoms with the "Patriot Act" or the farm policy that pushes small farmers out and rewards corporate soil destruction, yet I pay my federal government taxes. Nor do I support the Connecticut Supreme Court decision on the Shepaug River.

The municipal water company in Waterbury, under an agreement signed in 1922, diverted water from the river for the city's needs. But between normal low water in summer and the water company's diversions, the river ran so low that fish kills were frequent and the whole river ecosystem suffered. Washington and Roxbury, two towns that the river flows through, the Steep Rock Association, and the Roxbury Land Trust decided to sue Waterbury, and pledged $3,000,000 dollars toward legal costs.

After a long Superior Court battle, Judge Beverly Hodgson decided in favor of Washington, finding that Waterbury had violated the Connecticut Environmental Protection Act, which states that "the air, water, and other natural resources are subject to the public trust to be protected from unreasonable pollution, impairment, or destruction." The judge prohibited the city from diverting water from the Shepaug and operating its water supply system unless it met certain conditions, which included increased water flows to the river. She also found that Waterbury's withdrawals violated the riparian rights of downstream landowners and communities. In addition, she ruled that Waterbury violated its 1921 contract with Washington by selling water to towns around Waterbury and by diverting Shepaug water even when Waterbury's reservoirs were full, which it did because, to use its reservoir the water had to be pumped uphill into the system, but the Shepaug water was gravity fed and needed no pumping.

Waterbury appealed, claiming that its diversion of the Shepaug was not unreasonable because it met the state minimum stream flow regulations, and the case went to the State Supreme Court. Washington argued that the stream flow standards only covered fish protection and were not an appropriate gauge of the river's overall environmental health. It also claimed that CEPA overrode other state environmental laws and that the stream flow regulations did not adequately protect the river. The Court held that if the river met the state standards, the impairment could not be unreasonable and reversed Judge Hodgson on most of the issues. The Supreme Court also ruled that Judge Hodgson relied on an improper standard for minimum flows in deciding that the Shepaug River needs more water to sustain itself.

As a final blow, the case revealed that the water company had not maintained its pipe system, which leaked vast amounts of water, and was another reason the company took so much from the Shepaug River. The reversal ruled that Waterbury must repair its pipe system, but the city later declared bankruptcy and the State Legislature voted to cover the costs. So the company got its water system repairs paid for by Connecticut taxpayers, even while it was permitted to continue taking water from the river.

However, the inferior standard set by the Department of Environmental Protection for minimum flows, which the Supreme Court said were in place and must be observed, were exactly what led to the depraved state of the Shepaug to begin with. In like reasoning, would the court have us now comply with outdated standards for tobacco use, asbestos, hazardous waste disposal, or civil rights, which have become inadequate and have been updated?

Yet I still send the state my taxes.

I write letters to officials and to newspapers in my search for redress and to express my voice. But I'm not hopeful that enough people feel the same way for anything to happen. I know, though, that if our whole town and the town of Roxbury had the same courage as you, Henry, and collectively agreed to withhold our tax payments to the state that the river would benefit.

So Henry, I ask you: What are we to do? What is left for us who feel the power of finance can be toppled only by the power of greater finance? What about the currency of men's souls, Henry? Can we awaken enough of it in ourselves to recognize and claim as kin the right to enough water for rivers, enough trees for forests, or enough fish for the oceans? When will we realize that our choices every day contribute to the erosion of our lives, that our affluence deprives us of our wealth? Henry, it's a confusing world we live in, and an ironic one.

Henry, you said, "That government governs best which governs least" and assumed our wisdom to let well enough alone.

But we haven't left the river alone. We built a dam and a tunnel under Bantam Lake to divert the river for Waterbury, which certainly impairs the river's ability to heal itself. But the river has no recourse. It can't refuse to pay its taxes.

What if that government takes from the rights of rivers, animals, trees, air, and soil to enough clean water, clean air, and clean earth to sustain themselves?

We hear that these actions are often taken for "the greater good." You see, Henry, the river's flow here is symbolic of our faulty thinking (and acting based on that thinking) everywhere. Is water to be exploited merely because we can channel it into pipes and pump it elsewhere? Would we do the same with the air if we could? Is our increasing consumption of bottled water just the first step in the abandonment of clean drinking water from local sources? Or will water follow the marketing plan that our nation's food has—centralized by agribusiness and needing to be shipped long distances to all consumers?

You see, Henry, knowing the truth has not dissolved my fear. Nor has it set me free. Instead, it has made me a worried man. The truth expressed by the Supreme Court of Connecticut has abbreviated not only the rights of the river but also the rights of those who would defend it.

From where I sit I can watch the river level fall. It drops further each sun–baked day this autumn, all current gone now. In many places, the river, as a band of moving water, has vanished. Only fields of cobbles, scorched white by the sun, connect the isolated pools. The river is not polluted, yet that will come, as the first step in degradation is deprivation.

And now, much as in your day, Henry, the world swirls with contention, and conflict is imminent. In the face of all this, to withhold my taxes seems a small thing. I wish I had your courage, Henry.

Meanwhile, the river waits.

Little Lights

September 2003

I couldn't sleep last night and got up to get some milk and crackers. In the dining room I came face to face with a pulsing green eye. It took me a while before I realized that our younger son had left his laptop computer in there on the trunk and that the slow green pulses were an indicator of a computer in sleep mode. I was glad that at least the machines in our house were getting some rest. The green glow was bright enough to dimly light up the room, and I made my way to the kitchen without having to hold my hands up in front of me so as not to bump into anything.

This light is just the latest in a series of small lights that have come to reside with us, and I wonder if we aren't fooling ourselves sometimes with all the new conveniences they come attached to.

The lights from the internet modem and router in the living room combine with the standby light on the flat-screen TV. Together, there's enough light to play cards. There's also an electric toothbrush in the bathroom with a green charging light bright enough to illuminate the room. The clock on the microwave floods the kitchen with a neon blue light so bright I had to put painter's tape over it. Even then, I can see just fine in the kitchen at night.

Many of the devices that have these indicator lights aren't ever really turned off, but rather lie in a state of perpetual readiness, eager to come alive the instant we push a button. Waiting for the TV or stereo to warm up takes too much time. I heard on the radio that if all of these devices were truly "off" we'd save twice as much electricity as the Hoover Dam generates each year. That's a lot of power being used to prevent us from barking our shins in the dark.

Perhaps these lights are rooted in our need for quick results. But as we gradually spend more time indoors, the outdoors and its nighttime may seem to us more foreign and less comfortable. The need to keep it at bay may be served by these little night-lights. Did we ever get over our fear of the dark? Have we learned to enjoy it?

Maybe there's another fear operating here, a deeper one. John Muir once said, "The sun shines not on us, but in us," reminding us of our internal light and the need to stay conscious of it. There's a map of North America at night, as seen from a satellite, which graphically shows just how much darkness we've eliminated from the night sky. Is the artificial light we fill the darkness with compensation for what light may be lacking inside us? Is it symbolic of what we'd like to ignite within ourselves? Can the proliferation of artificial light be taken as a sign of our desperation in this effort? Will we have to flood every corner with beams in order to feel secure? When we do, will we?

Perhaps the frenzy in our fear can help us see the need for darkness as a reminding stimulant for the growth of our own inner light. Like a blind person whose other senses have been heightened by lack of sight, the night and its darkness serve to keep our inner lights alive.

The old clock in our living room is driven by two weights

hanging beneath the dial and have to be hoisted every five days or so. The clock doesn't even have an illuminated dial because it doesn't need to; it chimes on the hour and half hour. The tone is a mellow sound, like the note on a xylophone. If I wake in the middle of the night, its chiming tells me what time it is and provides a sense of comfort, helping me get back to sleep. Moonlight on the kitchen floor reassures me also, and I lament the loss of its beautiful and varied glow as I walk through the all–too–well–lit darkness toward progress.

The Winter Wind in Your Face

January 2004

It was four below zero Saturday, yet there we were, up at 6:00, in order to be out the door by 7:30, in order to make it to the ski area when the lifts begin operating, at 9:00. We're organized, but getting four people in the car with all the right number of skis, boots, poles, lunches, jackets, hats, mittens, goggles, helmets, and other gear is a test, especially considering we like to have breakfast first. Yet we knew there were lots of other people doing the same thing at their houses in the predawn darkness, who would also be at the ski area when we got there. Skiing, as expensive and energy-consuming as it can be, still inspires people to overcome considerable challenges to enjoy it.

I started skiing with a long pair of wooden skis without metal edges. I wore a pair of square-toed leather boots with laces, which attached to the toe piece of the ski with leather straps. A cable rear binding kept my heel from slipping out. My bamboo ski poles had baskets the size of dessert plates. My neighbor had a hill that was free of trees but had a stone wall about two thirds the way down with an opening where there was once a gate. I pushed off, using every ounce of strength to control my barreling speed and thread that slot. I didn't always make it, but when I did, I felt triumph unlike any other.

I've read recently that the number of skiers is remaining flat, not growing with the population. It may be due to the aging boomer generation or to the high cost of running a ski area, or both. Many small, more affordable ski areas have closed, and the larger remaining ones are more expensive. With fewer areas, there is often crowding. A Vermont ski area I visited had a lift line so long an employee in a lifeguard chair read jokes to us through a megaphone as we wound our way through the interminable maze. Maze is a good word for that lift line, because I felt like a rat in a lab. That's not what skiing is all about. But it's what a lot of skiers are getting now and they deserve better.

Some ski areas have gotten so large that they expand to the next mountain in the range or even the one beyond that and then tie them all together with lifts. Just getting from your car to the slope at areas this big can require a shuttle bus trip of considerable distance. Skiers spend a lot of their day riding these connections, which is just fine with management. The more skiers there are in the air on lifts or in the lodge eating or in the shops buying means there are fewer of them actually skiing, where they might run into one another and cause annoying accidents.

Carrying heavily clothed people uphill with their skis on is not an easy task, and in the early days the areas didn't try to. You got pulled up the slope by a rope tow, poma lift, J–bar, or a T–bar. With those lifts, you got your exercise on the way up the mountain, too. Riding a T–bar with someone you didn't know required a level of cooperation not needed on a chair lift. We need more contact of that nature with our fellow humans. Most lifts now are chair lifts, and some are high–speed quads or even six packs. They can pour people onto the mountaintop way in excess of what the trails can safely accommodate. On some slopes, it's like being in a very crowded swimming pool—there's no room to swim, or to ski. Add to that the fact that skiers are still getting down the mountain faster than they're getting up it and you can see why a scene like the siege of a castle awaits you at the bottom.

But even with the crowds, ski mountains can sometimes, like the beach and its mob, provide solitude. The mountain, like the beach, is one place you can go to be a kid again. Also like the shore, the mountain provides the distant view that gives us a feeling of adventure in a world full of possibility. To its credit, management has done much more recently to meet this need for greater adventure. Terrain parks provide jumps and glades offer downhill routes through trees, both within ski area boundaries. Even skiing up the mountain with skins on the bottom of your skis is permitted now at some areas. The jumps, rails, and half pipes provide challenges that skiers used to have to invent. Glades are a throwback to skiing's beginnings, when there were no trails.

Even with some skiers on the trail, it's still possible to get lost in the rhythm of turning down the slope. That rhythm can be so fluid and absorbing that it gives you the feeling that the mountain is moving under you, a sublime experience that ignites skiers to seek more of it.

Then there's the simple beauty of the snow. Nature has altered our reality for us and it's there to enjoy. From the leafless, drab, muted landscape of November to the dazzling brilliance of a foot of new snow, a new playground beckons. Playing in it, you feel like a kid again. You sleep better at night. Tension fades. The hot chocolate enjoyed with friends or family in the lodge provides a cozy sense of connection. The day's exertions burn calories. In our country, where two thirds of us are overweight and one third of us are obese, we need to get out and be active in winter.

The temperature on that sub–zero morning rose to over 20°, and we carved easy turns in the packed powder under a piercing winter sun. The early rising, the preparation and packing of lunches and the car, and the long ride to the mountain came to mind.

But when I skied that slot in the stone wall as a 12–year–old, I bet on myself and I won. For another chance to do something like that on a slope, I will always return to the mountains in winter.

The Nature of Play

October 2005

In our efforts today to help our children develop self-esteem, we've given them so many opportunities prepared for them that I wonder if we haven't taken from them the experiences of making opportunities for themselves, which are, after all, the true root of confidence. It's one thing to perform well in an endeavor that someone has set up for you but quite another to achieve at one you've created for yourself. In the former case, you're striving toward someone else's standards, while in the latter the standards are your own. The nature and pursuit of play, as it's now practiced, is a case in point.

We had our sons' soccer teammates over on Saturday afternoon for a post-season party, and the degree to which they initiated and guided their own entertainment was refreshing, reaffirming my sense of hope in free play. All autumn long they'd striven for a winning season under the watchful eye of their coach, their matches full of the tension of competition and the expectation of performance. But left to themselves, they fell right into an informal soccer game on the lawn, during which they laughed together in genuine friendship. When they came in for pizza, they joked good-naturedly about their maneuvers on the field.

When I was in elementary school, we had no organized sports except for Little League, which everyone tried out for in the spring. Tryouts were a nerve-wracking time, because you really were separated by ability according to how the coaches saw it, and, like it or not, it did come down to a test of your personal worth, or at least that's how the kids saw it. The prize was to make a team, any team, in the major league. The minors were where anyone not good enough for the majors ended up. The season was short, and the games were full of friction. Coaches would let games continue under protest, if they felt the rules had been broken. Angry parents in the stands would yell at the coaches for not providing the greatest advantage to their sons. Winning was important, and it showed at game's end, when the losers wore the face of tragedy and the winners gloated. Players, parents, coaches, and umpires all went home drained.

George Bernard Shaw once said, "We don't stop playing because we grow old. We grow old because we stop playing." But he wasn't talking about participating in organized sports. Unlike playing, organized sports are more like performing, because there is a script to follow for most athletes and they're judged (both individually and as a team) on how well they execute that script.

True play is inventive and expressive and requires fluid creation. It is more than mere execution of skills. My Little League experience was mostly performance with little invention involved. The degree to which we find activity playful is the degree to which we are free to make choices and thereby express ourselves. On a baseball team, the pitcher exercises the most choice in deciding what pitch to throw. The batter has a certain amount of choice when he chooses what pitch to swing at or what field to hit to. The fielders really don't have much choice. Their script tells them to field the ball and get the out or prevent runners from advancing. At the game's beginning we can predict the ending—there will be a winner and a loser, as determined by the score.

When four-year-olds play, at blocks or the marble race or Legos or trucks and cars, they are free to choose at nearly every moment. There are no rules or scripts telling them what to do, and by its very nature, they are required to create in order to proceed. When we played in the woods and along the streams as kids we were equally unbounded by preordained goals. Our purpose wasn't neatly defined but spurred more by curiosity than anything else. What was under this rock? How many times could you skip a stone across the water? What was on the other side of the hill? Where did this path come out? People might call this exploring, not playing, but it's play too. And that's the point. Playing *is* exploring and involves choice and invention. The only "score" is measured by your level of enjoyment or discovery, or, better yet, wonder.

In every organized sport I can think of, there's an active challenger, a person or a team, representing the opposition, whose performance yours is compared to. True play involves a challenge, invented by the player, which is what also keeps his/her interest. Sometimes the challenge is conscious and sometimes it's not. When the challenge is too easy, it's made more difficult to maintain interest. This too requires invention and creation.

People develop, grow, and pursue life with vigor by finding out what holds their interest. Cultivating curiosity spurs purpose through finding meaning. Life with purpose is life enriched with self-esteem. This is what we seek for our children. It is a noble desire and one often best served, not in planned activities but in the life of the individual child. Without the passion of curiosity, there is no life. As Shaw might have said, "We grow old when we're just not interested any more."

Around the Lake, Around the World

June 2006

I biked around the lake nearby one evening recently and was struck by how differently I saw the same scenes I'd ridden past dozens of times. Although I traveled the same route, it wasn't the same ride, but instead a journey of detail and surprise, a trip of new connections. Where had I been that I hadn't seen them before? What had happened to cause me to see them now so differently?

On the first Saturday in June an hour before sunset, I headed out from our house upstream along the river, then across the village main street to the road to the lake. As it was my first ride of the season, I looked for a landmark from last summer and was comforted to find it: the patch of wild red columbines clinging to a roadside rock face. When I found them, they gave me the reward I sought: a moment of wild beauty I know no motorist whizzing by ever sees.

The route soon intersects a highway, and to cross both lanes I try to find a gap in heavy traffic going each way, without unclipping from my pedals. The contrast between the roads is alarming, as within a few seconds I've gone from a virtually vacant street, where I notice wildflowers, to a deafening highway of cars and trucks, where I cling to the guardrail to avoid speeding vehicles and struggle to keep my balance in their wake. It's not even a mile, but I'm relieved when I turn off onto a quiet side road that passes a cornfield and a pond.

I take a long slug on my water bottle as I approach a familiar sight, a plywood shack. But it's as if it's the first time I've seen it, although I've passed it many times. It doesn't even have the requisite tarpaper stapled to the bare plywood. There is no lawn; the woods come to the doorstep. A metal stove pipe pokes through the shingled roof. In the dirt parking area is a rusted pickup truck and, leaning next to it, a Harley with tassels hanging from the handlebars. Within a half mile are lakefront estates priced in the millions. How had I not seen this contrast before?

After a short rise, I drop past the small pizza restaurant to the lakeshore road where it passes the empty town beach. Two fishermen in a canoe and one standing on a rock cast into the lengthening shadows. At the cove around the corner, another mega house has gone up on the site of what used to be a dance hall called The Casino. During its heyday in the fifties and sixties it drew crowds in boats and cars from all over. When lakefront land was fully developed, builders took to the unprotected ridgeline above it. Two oversize houses that perch conspicuously on the crest now break the previously pristine ridge. When I spoke to a builder about how crowding was ruining the serenity of the lake he said, "You don't own the view."

"You're right," I replied, "we all do."

I pass more new oversize houses with lawns sweeping toward the lake, and around the next corner is a feeder creek from Ash Swamp, where I've seen wild trout finning.

A little farther on, the road becomes a causeway between the lake on one side and a small pond on the other. This dual access makes it a favorite fishing spot, and this evening it's crowded. Seven beat–up vehicles are crowded in and around a slot that holds three. The fishermen are all black or Hispanic, although there are no black families that I know of in this town of four thousand, and few Hispanic ones. There is much chatter in the flurry of rods and flying bait.

In contrast to this hum of activity, just 30 yards across the road, I hear the murmur of a foursome of golfers, all white, putting out on the 17th hole at the private lakeside country club. The two scenes, so close together yet realities apart, portray a world of gaping differences in human experience, far more than the six degrees of separation between us that is so often cited.

After the longest straightaway of the ride, I pass the largest public space on the lake, the state park campground, with adults sitting around campsite fires talking, and children off in the grass throwing Frisbees or blowing dandelion seeds. There are fishermen and women here too, but none are black. The sandy swimming area, which our young sons used to call Goose Poop Beach for obvious reasons, is empty.

A few curves later, I climb a slight rise to a surprising sight. A small, growing maple tree has split a card–table–sized rock wide open, a stark reversal of the usual scene, in which the sharpened stone axe cuts and splits the standing oak. This example from nature's world of perpetual competition reminds me of how strongly plants contend, and not just among themselves, for light and water. Indeed, they are the first agents in the cycle that eventually sends rocks to the sea as sediment. Immense soft power lives in many forms.

In the forest across the street, cattle graze beneath the shady canopy, a juxtaposition of two incongruent elements that I now see for the first time. Previously, in my mind's eye, I either saw deer in a forest or cattle in a field. Why do I see what's really there now when I hadn't for dozens of rides before?

In a field just a bit farther on, beyond the stone wall they've been restoring, a group of Latino masons play soccer in their work clothes. Their laughter and calls to one another remind me—the playground at recess. The contrast of their adult work and their youthful joy brings to mind a paraphrase of Picasso—"It took me my whole life to learn how to play like a child."

Around the corner, these joyful men are further contrasted with a couple, wearing sunglasses, reclining in lounge chairs on the private beach of a palatial inn, holding huge glasses of wine, gazing at the sun setting over the water. Around the next bend is a scene from younger age play: two boys and one girl at the rope swing, anxiously chatting and jockeying for the screaming launch and the centrifugal arc.

Leaving the lake, I pass the pizza house again, now abuzz with festive dining. Furiously pumping up the short hill and then down, succumbing to the siren of speed, I fly by the plywood shack. Then comes the focusing entrance to the busy highway, crossing oncoming traffic once again. On the slight downhill straightaway I race to escape this roar of traffic, pushing the cyclometer to 25. I turn onto the quiet stretch looking for the columbine, now on my side, and again savor a moment of wild beauty. I cross the river, plowing through a screen of gnats hovering over it and fish them out of the back of my throat with my tongue.

Then, in quick succession, the firehouse, the school bus garage, the recently renovated but now defunct restaurant, then the village and the quick chicane—a left at the bookstore, a right at the gas station, weaving through traffic to join the river again and race it to the homestretch. Crossing the invisible finish line at the mailbox, I lean back, no hands, and coast. Seventeen miles in a little over an hour, during which I've seen the mundane transformed to the sublime.

My questions are:

What occurs in your mind when you suddenly see the familiar as revelation, the forming of heretofore–unseen connections?

And even more important, how do I remain open to this sense of wonder?

A Trip to the Zoo

August 2013

We went to the zoo the other day and except for the tense, city driving, we did fine, until we got to the easy part, getting off at the right exit. After we missed the exit, we got off the highway to turn around and found that doing that wasn't so easy either. We stopped for directions, and the two people that I asked disagreed on how to go, so I asked a woman up the block who admitted that she didn't know how to get there. It turned out that the zoo was just around the corner. So much for a small world.

The sign over the entrance gate cheered us up right away. It said: "The Bronx Zoo: 252 acres, 3500 animals, 280 people dedicated to them."

Once inside, we started to learn things right away. The zoo is no longer a city of wire cages holding different animals. Instead, the animals are free to roam in habitats like their natural ones. Some habitats are forested, others are open fields, still others have dense bush. The design works well to keep the animals from a well–intended but pressing crowd. They can either approach or retreat, depending on their comfort level. But it is *their* preference. Try as we might, we didn't always see the creature, a sign that the animals really can exercise this choice. They're grouped by continent, too, which not only provides an authentic scene for the humans, but also might even furnish some of the animals with a sense of home. Or so you'd like to think.

Accompanied by our two children, we headed for the Children's Zoo, which we discovered is a wonderful assortment of activities grouped by theme as well as some great child-level critter viewing. The kids enjoyed exhibits that allowed them to hear like a rabbit, see like an owl, or hop like a frog or a wallaby. There were logs to crawl through and tree houses to climb to (with a slide to come down). There was even a screech owl in a cactus that they had to climb up a ladder to see.

We took a cable car to the other side of the zoo to see Africa, where we learned that there are three kinds of zebras, a hairy rhinoceros, and one type of deer (the only one) that doesn't shed its spots as an adult. We learned that the difference between deer and antelope is that deer shed their antlers and antelope don't. We also discovered that there are 30 different kinds of mongooses and that the ones we saw, the meerkats, are known for the sophistication of their social behavior. They actually babysit for one another and perform other group-related functions, much like dolphins and whales. This trait is notable in itself, but even more remarkable when you learn that they do such social activity for each other for up to a whole day, a great sacrifice for an animal that needs to eat every ten minutes.

The elephants we saw were eating, as were just about all of the other large mammals, and we were reminded of just how much territory it takes for them to support themselves. The giraffes are fed 45 pounds of grain and hay a day, the elephants twice that much. The elephants wash each meal down with 20 gallons of water. It takes a lot of biomass to support life that consumptive. But they had more than enough until Europeans appeared.

Everywhere in the zoo there was a strong message of

preservation. One standing sign reminded us of how many species have become extinct in the last 400 years and how many become extinct each decade. The difference in the numbers pointed out just how quickly extinction is accelerating. Most scientists agree that the number of life forms being eradicated right now in the rain forest is unknown. They haven't had the time, just ahead of the bulldozers, to count them. As another sign informed us, the rain forest is being clear-cut at the rate of 25 acres a minute to provide mahogany and other specialty woods for markets in Europe and the U.S. That's nearly two square miles a day. I read the sign and thought of the mahogany plywood that the installer is laying underneath our new kitchen floor.

Rhesus monkeys, the ones that gave us our blood type prefix, were imported into Europe and the U.S. during the 1950s for medical research at the rate of 100,000 annually. In 1980, field biologists estimated their total population at only 180,000. Still, 20,000 are imported for research annually. Another sign illustrated the decline of the elephant population, from 1,200,000 in 1980 to 600,000 in 1990. This sign was in front of the skeleton of a 35-year-old elephant that had been shot by poachers. The bones lay in textbook anatomy fashion and were perfectly intact except where the poachers had chain-sawed the tusks off. Despite such carnage, the major cause of killing is not poaching, but habitat destruction.

The zoo does not merely provide custody for its animals but is actively engaged with governments around the world to establish sanctuaries and maintain or increase populations of those creatures considered endangered. It's an outreach program with nothing short of global goals and has achieved considerable success. It has even been the breeding ground for species that are extinct in the wild, with successes reintroducing these zoo-born creatures back into the wild and reestablishing wild populations.

Saving wild animals from extinction is much more than a well-intended exercise in preservation. The humans that also inhabit this planet can't thrive without the biome that brought them forth, although many of them don't realize this fact yet. Thankfully, those who do have the foresight and determination to work toward restoration of the biome for all beings' sakes. It has been correctly noted that the only species that could be removed from the planet and not have any effect is Homo sapiens. After all, we appeared here last.

Small Farms

September 2013

The *Old Farmer's Almanac* tells us that we've lost over a million farms in the last 25 years, down from just over three million to an even two million. Lots of people are worried about that statistic and for a lot of good reasons.

Some farms are simply abandoned because they became unprofitable, but most farms are lost to developers for housing complexes or shopping malls or are absorbed by corporations that want to control the supply of their raw material.

The articles about this change warn of the dangers that the land is facing as small family farms disappear into large agribusinesses, where the "farms" are in the thousands of acres. Crop production on such a large scale requires tons of chemical fertilizers, which make the soil so dependent on them that it loses its ability to grow much without them. Soil structure is also destroyed, leaving a powder that is merely a vehicle for carrying added chemicals, and it either blows or washes away. The crops themselves are also so genetically altered for volume production and shipping that they've lost their ability to resist insects and need pesticides to protect them.

People also worry that our food supply will end up controlled by a few corporations, a situation we're headed for and which has a frightening potential for abuse of both customers and the land.

The farmers and laborers on the small farms are also disappearing. What's become of the millions of people that ran those million farms? Do they still have the dignity that goes with the honest labor of farm life? What happens to all that farmland? Is it absorbed by larger farms, or "developed"? Is the soil safeguarded and nurtured? I'd like to think so, but I don't know, and the almanac doesn't tell us about them.

We all have a picture of an ideal farm and the thought that it might not even remotely match something in real life is disturbing. I visit a friend of mine who runs a small farm in Vermont and when I'm there I like to get a bottle of raw milk, the kind that still has what makes it milk in it before processing removes it. But a new regulation by the state health board prohibits farmers from selling it any more. Although you may know your picture of farm life is glorified, even any shadow of it is passing from sight.

Usually, farms are sold off to meet debt or because it's too hard to make a profit, but selling out is always a last resort. It's not like the small farmer wants to cash out or see a new mall go up. There often is not much choice.

There weren't any dairy farms where I grew up, but my mother used to take us to a small stand where we bought apples and peaches that were grown in the 30–acre orchard behind it. In the spring, the trees were covered with blossoms in a sea of billowing white clouds, their scent sweetening the breeze. At harvest time, the smell of the cider press and the vibrant color of the fruit filled the shed. You could get whole baskets or pick from the bins and fill paper bags that were stacked all around. The farmers' children weighed your fruit in a scale that hung from a rafter, and you'd watch the big needle leap from zero to find the weight. The hand crank on the register didn't get used much because the cash drawer was always open anyway.

The last time I went by, the orchard had become a condominium complex. The adult in me knows that people need housing and that the orchard had become worth more in money for houses than for apples or peaches. But there are values more important than money, which are ecological, spiritual, and cultural, and to the small boy clutching a bag of fruit, there was no prize greater than the crisp fizzle and juicy gush of a bite into fall's first apple.

On Our Concept of "Development"

November 2015

When we think of the idea of economic development, we envision greater human presence and influence in the world through use of natural resources to create wealth and fuel growth. Development connotes positive change, with the potential to enrich our lives and sometimes those of others. We see land as economically valuable only if we sacrifice it to promote this growth. We assume that development implies betterment. And that the land is ours to sacrifice.

We believe that land changed by us to meet our needs has been improved with this "development." When we read of a developer's plan to build a new housing tract, "improvement" is what we have in mind. When further acreage is cultivated, although it might extend a crop's monoculture or require the draining of a wetland, we think "progress."

When we "develop" land, every action we take undermines that land's capacity for production of oxygen and soil and for water purification, storage, and movement through the water cycle. The land, when we are finished "developing" it, is now diminished in its ability to live and to support other life. We have handicapped its health, and although we now more often use mitigation practices to lessen our impact, the net result is still a *loss* of that parcel's ability to support life.

What's more, when we're finished "developing" that land, not only have we removed land that was self–sustaining and highly productive, but we're also left with some type of building or road that requires consumption of even more resources (think, more land) to sustain it. In this way, the destruction of "development" is compounded—first with initial construction and then with subsequent maintenance and the needed consumption for that.

Our economy, operating under this concept of "development," relies on exploiting the wealth of our natural environment, taking land, forests, water, and soil, a process that exhausts the earth's ability to sustain life. We clear–cut forests, crippling them, instead of logging sustainably. We farm monocultures industrially, destroying fertility and losing topsoil We replace land and healthy ecosystems with housing, roads, and urbanization. We destroy rivers with dams and diversions, exterminating whole ecosystems, both wild and human. We pollute our earth's atmosphere with greenhouse gases, disabling climate balance.

Everywhere, our economy depends on this destruction and consumption, which produces only money, waste, and reduced capacity to sustain life. Even though we now know that we are consuming the planet's air, water, and soil faster than the earth can replenish them, the idea that land "development" is an improvement remains embedded in our relationship with the earth.

The word "development" as we currently use it about land not only misleads us but also subtly casts our destruction as benefit because it conceals what really happens and allows us to proceed in the comfort of our misconception. The economic *development* that fuels our financial economy is ecologic *diminishment* of the natural economy that supports us on this earth. Every housing tract, office building, road, dam, mine, clear–cut forest, or source of pollution weakens the globe's ecosystems. Every town's "Plan of Development" is really a plan of *diminishment* and should be so labeled. At least then we'd be forced to consciously confront our role in the permanent loss we were creating. With this honesty perhaps we'd be less destructive. We'd have to acknowledge exactly how much we were taking from the "commons"—the earth's supply of clean air, pure water, and healthy land.

We cannot continue to extract without replacing, cannot continue to remove without returning, cannot continue to spend the wealth of the natural world without restoring the health we have diminished.

We must move away from seeing the land as valuable only if we sacrifice it. We are blind to wild land's value, mostly because it is not monetary. We must realize that land, water, and air are far more valuable in services that sustain life everywhere. The disabling of these services results in climate change, desertification, rising sea levels, ocean warming and acidification, drought, wildfires, famine, floods, rising extinction rates, land and soil loss, political instability, and the crippling of earth's ability to sustain life.

What if we created an economy that provided enough for all while balancing consumption with replacement?

We must understand that when the land is valued and used kindly it can be preserved and still used well. We must move toward an economy of return.

The health of the soil and of the land can be kept with practices that restore to it elements removed by farming. Regenerative farms yield the same economic returns as do industrial farms, but use about one third as much energy. Prime arable land should not be used for housing. Housing should be clustered to reduce fragmentation of ecosystems. Fresh water can be preserved with storm water and point–source management and preservation of aquifers and stream levels. Clean air can be protected with the same attention to restoration. We can take fish from the oceans or trees from the woods and maintain the health of the stocks and the forests, but only at nature's rate of replacement. We can recycle much more of what we use. And we know what these practices are, have used them successfully, and are improving them.

All of these practices require limiting our consumption to rates that match nature's ability to replace or restore what we've used. Whether we will do this voluntarily is the question; the lure of short–term dollar gains spurs exploitation, not nurturance. We need to renew our exercise of restraint, which, as Wendell Berry writes, "is still a respectable human possibility. All it requires is the proper humanity."

A Wish for Winter

January 2020

It is 14 degrees this morning, and the river is frozen from both banks toward the center, the freeze forming a saw–toothed edge where it meets the current. A ribbon of slurried ice glides along this edge, imparting a barely audible scrape, the hushed voice of the water still moving. It murmurs of the impending closure of the stream's surface, transforming the river's public persona as movement incarnate, eternal change, to the stillness of sleep. But it's not sleep.

The ice cover is actually a quilt that the river pulls over itself to continue its work while resting. Underneath, the current still carries sediment to the delta, delivering mountains to the ocean. Brook trout, finning slowly in the depths, are dormant now, their eggs incubating in the riverbed gravel. Caddis flies cling to the rocks nestled in that gravel, slowly transforming from larva to pupa, preparing themselves for emergence with the earth's increasing tilt toward the sun. The trout have been doing this since the Laurentian ice sheet retreated 11,000 years ago; the insects began hatching a quarter of a billion years before dinosaurs browsed the tropics. The whole voice of the river goes from reminding us it is here to quietly whispering of its return. All this contraction is necessary for life to continue.

The only snow so far this winter, a few inches, fell a month ago and melted with the following rain. Temperatures since September have been above average, reaching nearly 70° twice last weekend. The year is on track to be the hottest on record. The earth's cooling system is disabled, brought to its knees by a surplus of carbon trapped in our atmosphere. In response, it convulses.

The effects worsen each year, producing a cycle in which extremes are the new normal. We look to the summer sky now not for the good rain but for the torrents of a biblical event. Extended droughts scorch regions. Formerly natural rhythms of wildfire have become nationwide infernos, charring 40,000 square miles in Australia and over 3,000 square miles in our country, with over 2,000 square miles of that number in Alaska. In addition, in 2019, humans deliberately burned over 7,000 square miles in the Amazon basin, an area over a thousand square miles larger than Connecticut. The 100–year flood became the 50, is now the 25, and is heading rapidly for the annual.

The writer Rebecca Solnit describes "the tyranny of the quantifiable, the way that what can be measured nearly always takes precedence over those things that can't: private property over public good, speed and efficiency over enjoyment and quality, the practical over the mysteries and meanings that are of greater use to our survival and to lives that have some purpose and value that survive beyond us to make a civilization worth having."

Solnit continues: "The destruction of the earth is due, perhaps in large part, to a failure of the imagination or to its obstruction, by systems of accounting that can't count what matters. The revolt against this destruction is a revolt of the imagination in favor of subtleties, of pleasures money can't buy and corporations can't command, of being producers rather than consumers of meaning, of the slow, the meandering, the digressive, the exploratory, the numinous, the uncertain."

Humans once enjoyed winter's gifts, having learned skills to live in balance with them. We see these gifts now as hardships, obstructing our impulsive rush to the next best thing, which has gotten us to where we are.

But we will face hardships far greater in order to preserve the health of our winter and of our home. The most difficult will not be just in how we travel, heat our homes, generate electricity, and produce goods and services. These changes are necessary and daunting, but they are, in the end, changes that are made "out there" in the physical world, and, even if achieved, they will still be insufficient.

We also need to make changes in what we value, in the way we see our place in the world: that the public good is often more valuable than private enterprise, that pleasures money can't buy or corporations can't command aren't free because they are worthless but because they are priceless, that the subtleties of wonder, love, laughter, gratitude, redemption, grief, and loss not only can't be measured but also have no need to be measured because they are what make us human, alive and connected. For this we will need to expand our imaginations beyond ourselves to encompass the whole of the suffering, beautiful world waiting for us to wake up too.

The Ghosts of Peaches

February 2020

I took some peaches out of the freezer this morning to add to my oatmeal and for a moment remembered the warm September morning when I picked them from the trees in our yard. These trees had originally sprouted in the garden, dropped there by the withered peach tree that hangs over it, before I transplanted them along the border of our yard. For 20 years the property line between our old neighbor and us was vague, lying somewhere within a mixed tangle of bushes and vines. For over 10 years, the seedlings grew, the last four producing dozens of luscious peaches.

The land beyond, about 10 acres, was a thriving meadow along the river. A copse of tall white pines stood in the distance, and groups of small birches, maples, and some old apple trees provided random clusters of shade. Larger beeches and maples bordered the river. Deer browsed and bedded in the tall meadow grasses, and monarchs fed at the milkweed, with other butterflies at the goldenrod and pokeweed. A fox denned in the island of small trees near the peaches each spring.

When the new neighbor moved in, the new survey line placed the peach trees two feet inside his side of it. Then the heavy equipment followed.

Nearly all the trees in the meadow were removed, including those along the river, their cooling shade taken with them. All ground cover was stripped and trucked away or burned in large fires. The topsoil was bulldozed, screened of rocks and the organic matter that makes it soil, and then spread out in layers of now inert powder.

The soil was crushed under the weight of machines, starting with the tree harvester and tree chipper, both on tracks, and the log skidder. One day there were seven excavators operating at the same time, along with two 10-wheel dump trucks, two bulldozers, two front-end loaders, and a screener. The work continued for over two months. With this pounding, the soil lost its channels for air and water, ingredients necessary for healthy plant growth.

The impacts from this are alarming.

The fox that denned in the meadow is gone. Deer no longer browse there. No hawks turn over the barren land, seeking moles, shrews, or voles, which are also gone. Swallows and nighthawks no longer spiral overhead. No bats flicker in the evening air; no thrushes or warblers sing. The owls that called from their roosts are all gone. Turkeys are gone. All ground cover is gone: goldenrod, milkweed, wildflowers, meadow grasses and brush. All insect life, above the earth and within it, is gone: butterflies, dragonflies, damselflies, fireflies, and all other pollinators.

Goethe said that there is nothing more frightening than ignorance in action.

The peach trees are gone too, replaced by a sterile, martial line of identical spruces. Before the workers sawed them down, I had picked and frozen as many peaches as I could, yet dozens still fell with the trees, their stored sunshine resplendent in the grass. The last of the frozen ones in my oatmeal this morning tasted bittersweet.

To Feed the World, Free the Rivers

March 2020

Right now, the U.S. is the world's largest food exporter. Also right now, the U.S. is losing 1,500,000 million acres of land a year to urbanization and road construction. That's 175 acres an hour, 3 acres a *minute*.

It takes nature 500 years, on average, to make an inch of soil, with deserts slower and tropics faster. Due largely to agricultural practices and development, the U.S. is also losing *soil* at a rate ten times faster than nature can replenish it, or about 3.6 tons per acre, per year. China and India are losing soil about 30 to 40 times faster than the U.S. Within 10 years, our increasing population will meet decreasing arable land and soil loss, and we will no longer have food to export, as the shrinking amount we grow will be needed here. We need to stem the loss of cropland and soil, restore as much of both as we can, and produce more food if we are to sustain ourselves, never mind the millions who depend on our food exports. Bristol Bay, Alaska, provides a path toward increasing food production.

The rivers of Bristol Bay now produce great quantities of sockeye salmon yearly in a sustainable fishery that supports about 15,000 well-paying jobs and contributes $1.2 billion to the local economy. In 2019, the harvest was over 235 million pounds of just *one* of five kinds of salmon. No dams obstruct the rivers of Bristol Bay, which is just *one* of four major commercial fishing districts, also without dams, each with dozens of rivers.

Our West Coast and East Coast rivers were once even more bountiful, not that long ago, before the wave of dam building that ended in the 1970s. Salmon runs to the Pacific, from California to Washington, provided thousands of tons of fish annually. Shad, sturgeon, Atlantic salmon and herring migrations on the Atlantic coast were just as prolific.

According to some estimates, there are as many as two *million* dams in the U.S., with more than 87,000 hazardous ones in the Army Corps of Engineers inventory alone. Between 75 and 90 percent are estimated to be obsolete. That's 1,500,000 dams that no longer serve any purpose, are unsafe, or cost more to maintain than to remove. But they are dams that are still killing fish.

On both coasts, where river dams have been removed, fish runs return. On the Elwha River in Washington salmon returned to their spawning grounds above two former dam sites within weeks of the dam removals, and the runs have increased each year. On Butte Creek, a Sacramento River tributary, dam removal turned a Chinook salmon run of 14 fish into a run of 20,000 11 years later. On the Kennebec River in Maine, the number of returning alewives jumped from 78,000 to 5,500,000 also 11 years after the dams came down. Rivers with the best–preserved watersheds have the greatest returns, but all runs increase when dams are removed. And there are other significant benefits to dam removal besides fish harvests.

Thousands of jobs are created removing the dams, thousands more in the removal of silt built up behind them and in replanting the thousands of acres of land formerly underwater. The removal of just the four dams on the lower Snake River, according to the Army Corps of Engineers, will create between

13,000 and 27,000 jobs immediately. And there are 227 dams at least 100 feet high, with over 400 dams in total, on the Columbia/Snake River system. A growing fishery on both coasts will create hundreds of other new jobs.

But the advantages don't stop with more food and jobs. When the keystone species return, the entire ecosystem rebounds. With increased acreage of forest, we increase climate change mitigation. Without dams, rivers return organic matter to the ocean, enriching marine nurseries. Restoring free–flowing rivers will also revive scores of communities that once lived interwoven with fish migrations in many regions of our country. Celilo Falls, on the Columbia River, the oldest continuously inhabited community in North America, was home at times to about 10,000 Native Americans for 11 centuries. It was drowned behind the Dalles Dam in 1957, a story repeated scores of times along our Pacific and Atlantic rivers.

We now know that dam removal succeeds in restoring ecosystems and economies. But we will only discover how much of our spiritual life lies stagnant behind dams when they are gone.

Lessons From Covid–19

April 2020

Everything about this New England spring is suspended, the natural world on extended pause, the human one as well. While blossoms remain in their buds, people self–quarantine in their homes. Humanity scrutinizes statistics on deaths and new cases, and the season here is stuck in late–stage winter: Fields lie in brown mats, trees skeletal, skies laden with steely clouds. Even the birds, which are beginning to arrive, are mostly silent in the frost–draped mornings. I bike around the lake into an icy northern wind that stacks the iron water into whitecaps and brings tears to my eyes. Yet there are other cyclists here escaping confinement, clutching handlebars too tightly to wave. So we tip helmets, passing in mutual release and foreboding.

Covid–19 has landed with an impact that rivets attention. Doing anything in public requires masks and gloves. We have now passed 40,000 deaths, often with 2,000 more each day. In nine days, we'll reach the casualty total for the Vietnam War. That rise is matched by the fall of the DOW, as the GDP contracts and the economy, as it's measured, crumbles. But our fixation on the financial economy, on growth at any cost, has, through our failed response, caused many of those deaths, the great majority belonging to poor, black, or Hispanic people, those among the over 60% of the country who have no Wall Street investments, even the many millions in the supposed middle class whose finances cannot absorb a $400 surprise expense.

America has now become a banana republic, complete with a dictator and his corrupt administration and a singular focus on one product: money. But money for only the right kind of people: white and male. And the plan has succeeded. Three white men, Bill Gates, Jeff Bezos, and Warren Buffett, now have more wealth than that of the bottom half of the country. This in a country in which raising the federal minimum wage, last set in 2009 at $7.25/hr., to $15.00/hr., is repeatedly defeated, despite the fact that, adjusted for inflation, the minimum wage should now be more than $22/hr. But the obsession with the stock market won't allow it.

Among the many changes that need to occur post Covid-19 is creating and governing by different metrics. Call those metrics our Whole Health Index.

Some suggestions for what we need to know each day about our *land*: How many acres of land were lost that day to urbanization and development, and how many were preserved or reclaimed? How much of our forest was clear-cut, how much conserved or replanted? How many miles of our streams and rivers were polluted, how many ran clean? How much wetland was filled in, how much saved or restored? How many square miles of our lakes, wetlands, and oceans were polluted, how many were clean?

We also need to know about our *people*: How much processed food and red meat are purchased each day, how much fresh produce, grains, and fish? How many meals are purchased at fast food chains, how many at healthier alternatives? How many people are exercising regularly, how many are obese? How many breathe clean air, how many don't? How many go to bed hungry, how many well fed? How many are homeless, how many sheltered? How many find freedom *in* their work, how many seek freedom *from* it? How many enjoy rewarding social connection, how many live in loneliness? How many self–medicate with alcohol, opioids, or antidepressants? How many are actively learning and engaged with life? How many are subjected to racism or sexism, how many truly equal?

If we fail to take stock of all that matters, with our governance and lives driven only by financial wealth, our current trajectory will remain in a coma, our culture rotting, our real wealth on life support, and in the not too distant future historians will write that America, once such a noble experiment, eventually became so poor that all it had was money.

The Worst Environmental Disaster
You've Never Heard Of

January 2021

The Pebble Mine, if permitted, would create the world's largest copper, gold, and molybdenum mine in the world. It would also destroy the world's largest sockeye salmon spawning run, the basis for a large part of Alaska's sustainable economy.

Exploratory drilling for indicated ore deposits began in 1988 in south central Alaska in the headwaters of Bristol Bay, the center of the state's salmon fishery. Since then, Northern Dynasty, the Canadian corporation making the proposal, has spent over $350 million on the Pebble project for engineering, environmental, and socioeconomic studies as well as other test drilling, prefeasibility studies, feasibility studies, and eventually, the permitting process, which began in 2012. The total cost of building the mine is estimated to be $4.7 billion.

Pebble is the largest known undeveloped copper ore body in the world. The deposit could produce up to eleven *billion* metric tons of ore. The largest existing mine, the Safford Mine in Arizona, has produced 7.3 billion tons of ore. The Pebble ore is low grade, which is what requires mining these huge amounts in order to ensure profitability.

The plan includes two sections: Pebble West, where the ore

is near the surface, which would entail open pit mining, and Pebble East, where ore would be extracted through underground methods. The open pit mine at Pebble West will be two miles wide and several thousand feet deep. Most of the rock removed will be waste rock. Up to 2.5 million tons are expected. This waste rock, along with allowed discharge chemicals and mine tailings, would be stored in two "tailings storage facilities" behind massive earth dams. The largest of the dams would be 685 feet tall and 4.3 *miles* long. Current design would also include the construction of a port on Iniskin Bay with a private two–lane freight road 86 miles long between the mine and the new port. Four pipelines carrying a slurry of metal concentrate from the mine to the port will be built along the road. Trucks will haul ore concentrate to the new port, with the ore and metal smelting to be done off–site. The project would employ over 1,000 people for the first 25 years of the mine's expected 45–year–life span.

According to a recent scientific study, Bristol Bay is home to the world's largest commercial sockeye salmon fishery and also has some of the largest runs of other types of salmon in the world. One of the seven major rivers draining into Bristol Bay, the Kvichak, supplies 50 percent of the world's wild sockeye salmon alone. The Chinook salmon run of the Nushagak River is among the largest in the world. Every year, 50 million salmon return to the rivers of Bristol Bay. The fishery supports 14,000 high–paying jobs and more than $480 million in annual economic activity.

The return of the salmon brings nutrients into the watershed and supplies terrestrial and aquatic food webs. Brown bear and moose are abundant in the drainages, and one of the largest caribou migrations, the Mulchatna herd, travels through the region. The area is also home to smaller mammals, such as otters, wolverines, porcupines, red fox, and mink. All are directly or indirectly connected to the health of Bristol Bay and its salmon.

Also strongly connected to the region are the indigenous cultures. The Yup'ik and Dena'ina are two of the last intact, sustainable salmon–based cultures in the world and have lived as a part of this land for at least 4,000 years. Of the 25 Alaska native villages of Bristol Bay, 14 are within the Nushagak and Kvichak watersheds. Thirteen of the 14 are federally recognized tribal governments. Over 50 percent of their subsistence harvest is salmon.

The Pebble Mine project has been a major issue in Alaskan politics since 2005, when the Renewable Resources Coalition was formed to oppose it. A raft of active legal, electoral, and legislative challenges to the project have been filed in Alaska since 2007. Some have been stalled permanently in legislative committee. A ballot measure, the Alaska Clean Water Initiative, introduced in 2008 and designed to outlaw large–scale mining in the Pebble area, was voted down at statewide polls, but the results were cast into doubt when, in 2009, the state's own Public Offices Commission released a report detailing violations of campaign funding laws during the voting. A poll of Bristol Bay residents reported 20 percent in favor of the project and 70 opposed. At six recent Environmental Protection Agency hearings in Bristol Bay area towns, 94% of participants voted in favor of having the EPA protect the watersheds permanently under Section 404 (c) of the Clean Water Act, which they are authorized to do.

The economic arguments for both sides have long been debated. Proponents contend that the project will provide significant tax revenue to the state; the opposition cites Alaskan tax structure, which shows that oil and gas drilling returns 20 percent of resource value to the state and municipalities, fishing returns between 1 percent and 5 percent, and mining returns 1.5 percent.

Mine proponents point to the creation of 1,000 permanent

jobs during the 30–60–year life of the mine; opponents highlight the 14,000 high–paying jobs already supported by the fishery.

Although projected estimates for the total worth of the extracted metals are placed at $300 billion, the cost of building the mine is estimated at $4.7 billion. Profits would also be huge. Northern Dynasty has projected the annual pre–tax cash flow at $2 billion for the first years of operation, and considerably more in later years. These projections have provided the incentive for the $350 million spent in preparation, even before the permitting process began. It is important to note that although the mine site is in the U.S., the mineral rights and the project are *wholly* owned by Northern Dynasty, a Canadian corporation, and all profits would flow to it.

In February 2010, Northern Dynasty released a report that stated the total measured and inferred resources of both sections of the mine at over 80 billion pounds of copper, over 100 million ounces of gold, and over 5 billion pounds of molybdenum. To extract these amounts of metal, the operation will mine about 10 billion tons of ore, which equals 200,000 tons *a day* for the 45–year expected life span of the mine.

On an equally large scale, the Pebble Mine presents environmental and economic hazards in both its construction and operation, as well as its life after mining has ceased.

The construction of the mine will block or eliminate between 55 and 87 *miles* of salmon spawning and rearing habitat in the watersheds of the most productive sockeye salmon fishery in the world. Water flow in an additional six miles of salmon rivers would be reduced by diversions required for the mine operation. To operate its pipelines and for other mining needs, Northern Dynasty has applied for water rights permits to Upper Talarik Creek and the Koktuli River totaling 35 billion gallons of ground and surface water per year, which is four times the annual water usage of Anchorage, a city of 300,000. According to the Environmental Protection Agency, roads would cross 34 streams, 20 of them known salmon streams.

In addition, 4,200 acres of wetlands would either be filled or excavated. Over 1,000 additional acres of wetlands would be blocked, lost under the road, or destroyed by silt or salt. This loss would reduce food resources for stream life, shift the balance of surface and groundwater, increase summer water temperatures, and decrease winter water temperatures.

There is another category of overall risks that describes those hazards resulting from a failure or multiple failures of dams, pipelines, and culverts. Using the historical record of dam failures, the probability of a dam failure at Pebble is estimated to be between one in ten thousand and one in a million. Dam failures can occur through overtopping (fluid coming over the spillway), seepage under or through the dam, or outright dam collapse, either partial or total.

The seismic risks to the dams planned for the Pebble project are difficult to quantify, but some facts are known. The Lake Clarke fault lies within 20 miles of the Pebble deposits and possibly much closer. The actual ground trace of the fault and its splays in the Pebble area are unknown due to extensive ground cover. The Lake Clarke fault is a western branch of the Castle Mountain fault. Recent studies indicate that a magnitude 7.1 quake can be expected to occur on the Castle Mountain fault on a 700–year cycle. The subduction zone that was the source of the 1964 Good Friday earthquake of magnitude 9.2 lies approximately 125 miles south of the mine site.

A dam's height determines the depth of the impoundment behind it and, as depth increases, the pressure on the dam also increases. The largest of the several earthen dams at the Pebble Mine site will be 685 feet high and 4.3 miles long. There are only a few dams in the world that are taller. None of them is a tailings dam. For comparison, the Three Gorges Dam in China is 606 feet tall, the Aswan Dam is 364 feet tall, and the Hoover Dam is 725 feet tall. An earthen dam comparable to one at the Pebble Mine is the Oroville Dam on the Feather River in California. It is 60 feet taller and 6,920 feet long. The reservoir behind it holds 1.1 *trillion* gallons of water. Quantities this large can be difficult to visualize, but, for a reference, the best example we might have would be the Deepwater Horizon well blowout in the Gulf of Mexico. By the time it was capped in July 2010, it had contaminated 491 miles of coastline, closed 4,200 square miles to shrimping, and affected over 68,000 square miles. It was the largest oil spill in history, at 210 *million* gallons. The largest of the Pebble Mine dams is over three times longer than the Oroville Dam and would hold over three *trillion* gallons of *toxic waste.*

Dam failures, though rare, are not unknown. The Teton Dam, an earthen dam on the Snake River in eastern Idaho, collapsed as it filled for the first time in June 1976, killing 11 people and 13,000 head of cattle; it also destroyed thousands of homes and businesses in five communities downstream. Although the area surrounding the site was highly fissured, permeable, and unstable (and, incredibly, built anyway, even with this knowledge beforehand), its collapse was not due to a quake.

According to a panel commissioned to investigate the event, the failure of the dam was due to the permeable soil used in the core of the dam, the fissured rock in the foundation of the dam, and "design decisions that permitted the failure to develop." When the dam failed, it released sediment–filled water. It was 305 feet high and 3,100 feet long.

The four pipelines and dozens of culverts planned for the Pebble Mine present failure risks that are more reliably calculated, because these failures have happened much more frequently, and their histories are much more extensive. Projected from historical records, there is a 98 percent chance that one of the four, 86–mile pipelines in the Pebble Mine plan will fail in 25 years. Given that the active life of the mine will be between 45 and 78 years, risk of a failure of this kind is extremely high.

Waste storage systems for mines have been in existence for only 50 years and, even over such a relatively short length of time, some have failed. Given that the ore at Pebble would be mined for decades and the waste would require management for centuries or even in perpetuity, the large scale of the mine and the long time required to extract the ore amplify these risks.

Even complying with all regulations, mining has a poor environmental track record. According to the U.S. Environmental Protection Agency, mining has contaminated over 40 percent of the watersheds in the western continental U.S. Decontamination of 500,000 abandoned mines in 32 states is estimated at 54 billion dollars. A recent study of 25 large, hard–rock metal mines compared water quality outcomes with environmental impact statement predictions from the permitting stage. Nineteen of the 25 mines exceeded water quality standards in releases to either surface water or groundwater. When the 15 mines with the highest acid drainage, contaminant leaching potential, and proximity to groundwater during the permitting stage are considered together, 14 of those 15 exceeded water quality standards. In other words, a higher risk of contamination during the study phase correlates to higher actual contamination after the mine has been built, even with strict regulatory compliance.

Many thought the Pebble Mine project was dead back in 2014, when the Obama administration's EPA preemptively vetoed it, using its authority under the Clean Water Act. However, under Trump, the EPA began a fast–track environmental review process of its own decision and, in August 2020, announced the results of that process. Reversing its earlier findings, the agency concluded that the project poses no serious risks to the rivers of the Bristol Bay watershed. That same month, Joe Biden announced his opposition to the Pebble Mine, citing the "rigorous, science-based EPA veto" made during the Obama–Biden administration.

All that was left for the project to proceed was for the U.S. Army Corps of Engineers to issue a permit, which they were expected to do after they had issued a positive Environmental Impact Statement in July.

However, in a surprise move in November, the Corps denied a permit for the project, stating the plan "does not comply with Clean Water Act guidelines" and that it had failed to mitigate "for all direct and indirect impact" to rivers in the watershed.

In another surprise move, Alaska's two U.S. senators, Lisa Murkowski and Dan Sullivan, strongly supported the Corps position.

In December 2020, Northern Dynasty announced it would appeal the Corps denial. If its appeal succeeds, the permitting process will proceed.

It's clear now that if the Pebble Mine is built, in opposition to over three quarters of Alaska's population, both its U.S. senators, the Environmental Protection Agency's original decision, and the Army Corps of Engineers, that Northern Dynasty would get very wealthy.

But it is also clear that the wealth of the sustainable salmon harvests, the health of hundreds of square miles of watershed, and the livelihoods of thousands of Alaskans would be destroyed.

What we do to the Earth, we do to ourselves.

Part Two
The Natural World

Incongruent Beauty

May 2005

A recent contrast comes to mind: in the foreground, the giant moth, at the airport window in Chicago, clinging to the cement sill and behind it the massive polished aluminum wings of the jets at their bays.

The moth was out of place, dwarfed by the planes, and except for a few pigeons the only natural life form within the reality of glass and steel and tarmac (and plastic–wrapped food) that is the airport. What can it find here to eat, I wondered.

It drew attention, passengers waiting for flights bending to look, tapping the glass to get a reaction. Through the double pane, the moth was as large as my hand and mimed its closing when it folded its wings.

I knelt and looked into its large black eyes and saw a being in transit to another world, a migrant perhaps, but not a comfortable one. Secretly, I wished it a safe journey to a more welcoming destination.

Its antennae were oval–shaped radar saucers, standing like rabbit ears. They stood above a face of brown fur with a white band across it, from which the dark eyes shone. What I could see of the body was cinnamon. But the wings were intricate, reminding me of a Persian rug, with woven patterns of black and tan, cinnamon and sienna. There were sets of eyes imbedded in them, one arresting pair larger than the rest.

"As a defense against predators," the man standing next to me said.

"Mimicry I think it's called," I replied.

In becoming something unappealing (or even frightening) to enemies, this moth had become a creature beautiful to behold, a larger than life figure in full command of my attention. It had done what was needed to preserve its own life and that of its species. Its size and grandeur were testimony to its path.

Behind the moth were the ranks of tethered aircraft, moored to the steel box gangways and tended with fuel lines, sewage lines, baggage conveyors, and trucks with scissor lifts loading food.

Yet within this gleaming, polished aluminum expanse of technology there wasn't the strength, power, or grace of this extraordinary moth.

Firebrands of Freedom

July 2005

There were fireworks last night, the muted booms and bright lights reaching us from the high school over a mile away. In the foreground, above our neighbor's meadow, floated a flotilla of fireflies, their pulsing lights swirling in a silent kaleidoscope of life and cyclical renewal. They were a silent invasion, having come not for war but to fulfill their biological destiny. In the driveway, our two teenage sons were lighting the collection of fountains and screamers they'd purchased at Walmart. Between the driveway and the high school displays there was enough noise to wake the dead. Or, we hoped, at least to wake the living. In mute independence from all the clamor were the fireflies, their silent flashes providing light continually and most noticeably when the manmade send-offs were not.

The scientists' term for the fireflies' ability to ignite is bioluminescence. The word practically rolls off your tongue— "Light of life." Once, when I was a boy, and I wanted to see if their glow would die with them, I killed one while it shone. And you know what? It continued to shine. In fact, I smeared the glowing thorax on a rock and painted an illuminated streak. I wondered, in my juvenile way, if the exercise of the scientific method was worth the bug's life. Such is the nature of an experiential education, or, in this case, experiential for the insect. It was more experimental for me but still left a vivid impression.

It is with the loud hoopla of fireworks that we celebrate our experiment with self–governance as a nation and proudly let the brilliance of pyrotechnics display our freedom and independence. (It is worth noting, however, that a rainy night will cancel them while the fireflies continue to flash.)

But what freedoms do we have to celebrate? In this year of the Patriot Act renewal, not as many as we used to. Are we free to read from libraries or buy from bookstores without concern for surveillance? Are we free to receive unbiased reporting from embedded journalists carefully placed in their war coverage to allow reporting only what they're shown? Are our women free to make their own reproductive choices? Are all of our citizens provided a sound, free education? Are all our citizens free from needing two incomes to pay a mortgage? Are our families free to be families, with children raised by parents instead of day care centers? (Give us fewer day care centers and the conditions that enable us not to use them.) The American dream has become a treadmill, and running upon it we trample our freedoms.

The fireflies merely go about their business, providing the gift of light in the process. Their glow comes not from tubes filled with rockets drilled in the ground but from a source they've created within themselves. They remind me of John Muir's remark that "the sun shines not on us, but in us." Their bioluminescence is rooted in their interdependence within the great web of the natural world, for which the web and they both serve a purpose.

We, as a nation, need to recognize this interdependence. First, we are dependent upon one another here in America to participate in the preservation and evolution of our freedom by staying informed and by voting. We need to see and understand "the other side" of the issues. We need to coach Little League, volunteer at the library, or serve on a board, commission, or committee. We need to write, call, or e-mail our representatives, senators, governors, and executives and voice our stand. We need to be part of the solution, working with other citizens to improve the quality of the life we share as a community and as a nation, not working solely to improve our bank balance.

We need to take more of our lives and our children's lives into our own hands. We need fewer surrogates taking responsibilities we should be handling ourselves. In a world of media celebrity, we need fewer life coaches and more discovery through action. We've given our freedom to decide our direction to a siege of influencers, social media algorithms, and advertisers.

To the many who allow so much of what they think about, buy, or act on to be decided by mass marketing or media, talk of freedom is moot. Freedom needs exercise to stay alive. It needs an individual at the helm, learning through the success or failure of deliberate choices and actions in the engagement of all our faculties: physical, spiritual, intellectual, emotional. It needs an awareness of and appreciation for this education. At the same time, freedom must recognize our interdependence, not just with our fellow citizens, but with all peoples and the entire natural world.

Until, like the fireflies, we live lives that are so bright, so completely engaged with all life that they continue to shine even when we're gone, our annual fireworks display will remain an empty ritual.

We can start right now—the fireflies are calling.

The Sweet Gum Tree Pod

June 2009

All summer the sweet gum tree holds its green balls of seeds unseen, camouflaged among its foliage. But with the first frost, the sweet gum launches its crop, and all of a sudden what you hadn't seen before is suddenly everywhere you look. The spent pods cover the ground, discarded by the tree that nourished them for so long.

Each pod, now brown, is a ping–pong ball of alternating spikes created by the explosion from within and the cavities the departing seeds were launched from: a shard of choreographed shrapnel having delivered its ordinance. The holes invite closer inspection. Like a rock with a promising exterior, they ask you to crack it open to see what's inside. It could just as easily be a medieval weapon or the death star from an intergalactic war. Which it might be if there weren't so many of them.

One tree, a single organism, may produce thousands of these pods, each with dozens of seeds, in a ratio that would seem far in excess of what is necessary for increasing the tree's population or even for simple reproduction.

Why so many? Perhaps the odds are long for any single seedling's survival. Perhaps the decaying pods help nourish the source tree. Perhaps the large numbers help ensure genetic variation to allow for adaptation to changes in the environment. For whatever reason, there's still the question—why all at once?

Is the release of so many at once required for the survival of the few? Or is the sweet gum tree, quietly cradling its resources, expressing its knowledge that there is to everything a season? The holes in the pods, left by the escaping seeds, echo those seeds' silent epitaph: *We were here, but were called by time to leave.*

Patagonia

I am standing in Coyhaique, Chile, over 3,000 miles south of the equator. In the foreground the rolling hills stretch to the wide-open vistas, the grass rippling in the wind. Clusters of small trees, stunted by the wind, hunker down in the clefts, where the slopes meet. Strong sun, clear blue sky. In the background, the Andes, slopes draped with snowfields, feed the streams that run west across the pampas, Atlantic bound. Vast distances span the basins, miles across the valley floors in the near-ground, the dirt road vanishing far, far ahead.

The mid-ground is where we fished, wading in where the streams hid themselves in the folds of earth, the double-track gravel roads leading to them contouring the hillsides, up and over, finally dropping to the water.

The water, a pellucid green pastel, slid smoothly over a colorful garden of rocks: tourmaline, burnt sienna, and white. The river, narrow with graceful bends, allowed views upstream a fair distance. It was rarely over your thighs. At the cut banks and overhanging bushes or trees, there were fish. They came readily to the fly, provided they hadn't seen you first. A light wind, stirring surface ripples, but not strong enough to derail your cast, helped mask your approach. But sometimes the air was still and your casts launched with the full expression of the rod, sending the dry fly to deliver its anticipation. The trout darted or cruised from under the cut banks, almost always taking the fly and then exploding, sometimes even onto the rocks or the banks, shaking wildly. Often they were successful, flinging the fly skyward and departing, a V wake behind them. Our guide, Norm Cousins, suggested that when you released them, you did so downstream. In their panic the trout would send their alarm to their schoolmates and spook the whole pool. Fear speaks in exclamatory sentences.

The flies we used didn't seem to matter much, as long as the sun was out. When my fishing partner, Stan Tucker, was casting foam hoppers and I was pitching stimulators, we both got strikes at the same rate. His fly had a smaller profile, and as the current got faster, it would float higher and longer than my deer hair fly. He switched flies more often than I did, but that didn't affect the strike number either. However, cloudy skies reduced the dry flies' effectiveness by a great deal. Suddenly, accurate drifts brought few, if any, strikes, and it was time to tie a nymph dropper fly beneath the dry fly to fish under the surface. Once we did, we started catching more fish, all of them on the nymph. This makes sense: without the sun's heat to stimulate insect hatching, there won't be any surface activity. Even the hoppers and beetles falling in from the high grasses decrease, as the lack of sun dampens their flight. We kept succeeding with the nymph (again, it didn't matter what nymph) until the sun returned and fish began taking the dry fly. If the sun stayed out, we got fewer fish on the nymphs and removed them. The warm rays ignited the insect life, more of which came to the top. We were back in dry fly paradise.

But as the wind rose, so did your casting challenge. Higher wind required shorter casts for control, but didn't make them easier, and, if inattentive, we snagged in the bushes. If a snag required wading to the bush to untangle the snarl, you gave up your turn, standing off to the side with your line out of the way so your partner could fish the remainder of the pool. I would nearly always snag my fly at the point when my casts had begun to close in on the sweet spot in the pool. Stan would take over and sometimes, but not always, he'd catch the large fish at the head of the pool. Our roles were reversed only rarely, until I improved.

Despite the strong incentive to cast safely in higher wind, you eventually had to drop the fly in the most promising drift, usually close to the bank or bush, within three inches from the target. These were small streams; small differences in the landing spot could make a big difference in response. The technique that evolved for me was to drive the fly with only one false cast, keeping the loop low and tight. Though demanding, and eventually tiring, it was necessary to avoid "casting out." It was either full focus with all abilities or I'd be giving my turn to Stan. I missed a chance at the largest fish of the trip with just such a miscast. While I stood off to the side, Stan took over and carefully worked his way to the head of the pool where he hooked and landed a fish over 20 inches long. He'd been nearly fishless all morning, and this one slaked his drought. I was glad for him, and more mindful of my casting. On my turn at the next pool I was so focused I caught six fish on six casts, trying to make up for the one I might have landed at the previous pool. In the morning, I gave up my turn more than Stan did his, but within a few hours we were even and the fisher who began the pool was the one most likely to finish it. Experience, as they say, is a strict teacher.

Sometimes my approach casts were without flaw but induced no response. Sometimes roots, hanging bushes, and small whirlpools encircled the prime target, and I sent the fly to the pinpoint touchdown, let it ride through the tangle of obstacles while biting my lip and feeding line into the drift, only to have it completely ignored. In disbelief, I sometimes managed to repeat the stunt, but still blanked. At this point, we'd almost always mutter "no one home" and wade up to the next riffle or run. This was particularly bittersweet when we reached the last fishable stretch at the end of our day and it was my turn. I flung my impeccably offered fly up into the most promising depths of a small canyon. I waded farther up, getting deeper into the recesses of the pool, sure that the leviathan I imagined would strike. Repeated accurate casts brought nothing, yet I was reluctant to concede to such a fate from a piece of water so prime and made more casts than I would have elsewhere. When I finished, I was satisfied that I'd done my best and was reminded that my role, though well played, was still only just one part of the combination needed to separate a trout from his home, even for just a few moments.

Even though I've been fly–fishing for fifty years, there are always new lessons. For one, I'd never fished before for five consecutive days, morning until evenings, and the sheer number of repetitions fostered rapid absorption and habituation of skills. By day two, I was reading the water in front of me more quickly and more accurately. A casting callous on my right palm that formed that day eventually hardened and is still quite prominent, two weeks after my return.

It is more than just hours of casting but doing so under the eye of a guide that motivates learning. I'd never been guided before, but I was experienced, and guiding is much more than taking you to the good fishing spots. Part of the unspoken expectation is that the guide will advise on fly selection and presentation as well. But the key question a guide must address is what advice is valuable *for this fisher* on this water, and when is it best given? The guide must determine what you don't know or don't know how to do and also know when and for how long he should provide suggestions. Not enough and the fisher flounders in his inability. Too much and the fisher won't develop the independence necessary to improve his skills. Our guide, Norm, was both plainspoken and balanced with his advice, and I needed and appreciated that.

Norm found one of my flaws right away. When fishing a dry fly, your dominant hand is holding the rod with the line underneath the index finger. As the fly drifts toward you, your other hand retrieves the line through the rod hand index finger. At the strike, the retrieving hand tugs downward to set the hook. If a hooked fish moves toward you, your stripping hand must be close to the rod to strip line fast enough to keep tension; if there's no tension, the fish will shake the fly.

Over decades, I'd developed a bad habit of dropping my retrieve hand to my side. When a fish struck, I'd quickly slide the line through my teeth for tension while also stepping backward, as if I could outrun the approaching fish in the opposite direction. The result was an off-balance retreat and lots of lost fish. "Where are your hands?" Norm would bark at me until, by the morning of the third day, keeping my retrieving hand near the rod was automatic, and I started landing more of the fish I hooked.

I had another bad habit of fighting a fish too long, which depletes the fish's oxygen and builds up lactic acid in its muscles. If a fish needs resuscitation at your feet after landing, they are near exhaustion and often won't survive such a loss of their reserves. Norm instructed me to play the fish until they stop running and can be turned, then lift their head out of the water and slide them into the net. Don't use a net with a small trout, but turn it belly up, which will immediately calm it. Even with a netted fish, turn the fish belly up to reduce its struggling while you remove the hook. If you lift any fish out of the water, for example, to take a photo, return them as quickly as possible to the water to improve their chances of survival.

The first goal is to release the fly from the fish, and to do so quickly. If you can, grasp only the fly and, with a twisting motion, unhook it. Use a hemostat for hookups deeper than the lip.

There are less important but still good reasons for landing and releasing a fish quickly. For one, you'll be spending more time fishing. Also, the more time you spend landing a fish, the more that struggle alarms other fish, reducing your chances for continued success. If you're worried that the knot to the fly will break with vigorous pressure, check it often and retie it if it looks worn. The leader almost never breaks, but knots that aren't monitored and retied break more often. I lost two memorable fish in Patagonia when knots broke. Don't undermine your efforts with weak knots.

Just as casting improves with all-day outings five days in a row, catching fish improves with repetition. One strategy aims for prioritizing fewer, but large fish over many but small fish. In water with a large number of wild fish, there will be a range of sizes and age groups. The largest fish will usually be at the head of the pool, where the current enters and they can station themselves in the best feeding position. Smaller fish vie for the feeding stations that are left, with the smaller ones usually at the tail of the pool. If you fish the tail first, you'll likely hook these smaller fish first and their exertions send the larger fish into hiding. To increase your chances for the large fish, skip the lower part of the pool and cast to the best feeding lie first. Norm called this "going for all the marbles." Your first cast must be good and you must be ready—you won't get a second chance, but this risk can be rewarding. Even if you hook and lose the large fish, your decision will have been confirmed. And if "no one is home" at the prime spot, you can restart at the tail and work the pool from the tail up.

A guide also needs to model correct technique for the client, and I learned much by observing skill applied in context. In this category, there was another important element of craft that Norm provided by instructing, "Don't fall in love with the drift." I was tempted, especially after I finally placed a long, difficult cast, to let the dry fly float longer than needed, but there's little pay–off in letting it float where it's been on previous casts. The long drift also caused coils of line to collect at my feet, which I would then have to return to the air on my next cast with lots of false casting, each time working more line out before finally releasing the cast.

Norm would watch me lay my full cast on the water and after only three or four seconds of the fly's drift would tell me to cast again, lifting the full length of the line off the water. I lifted the whole line off the water into the back cast and then laid it down again softly on the forward cast without any false casting. I thought this would drag the fly through the water and soak it, but I was surprised to find that it didn't. Instead, it allowed me to avoid false casting altogether. And, as the saying goes: "You can't catch fish if your fly's not on the water."

Norm monitored my improvement well and faded his cues accordingly, an important aspect of guiding. You won't become a better fisher if you aren't making your own decisions, and a perceptive guide will know when to fade one type of instruction and move to another focus. A competent guide will also know when to praise and for the right reasons. The simple phrase, "good cast," uttered at the right time, boosts confidence and motivates continued improvement.

As far away as it is, Patagonia is changing, and one of the reasons is the increased fishing traffic. More anglers are making the trip, and travel and access to the rivers have become easier. And even though we fished small streams and headwaters in the backcountry that the main lodges didn't, I saw boot tracks on the banks two hours' walk from where we parked. There was a car at our intended parking spot on two days, and we changed destinations. This may sound inconsequential, but the headwater streams are too small to accommodate two guided parties fishing upstream.

There are other indicators of more pressure as well. There were two pumping stations on the river near the airport, irrigating the adjacent fields, that Norm told us weren't there last year. When I asked if anyone monitored the stream diversions he said, "Trout are probably the last thing on a list of priorities." Five large-scale dam projects were defeated in the legislature, but others were approved, and some rivers will deteriorate. The Coyhaique downtown was being repaved, and a distinctive, higher-end shopping district is beginning to form. With 10,000 boomers retiring every day, traffic will only increase.

Even with these pressures, Patagonia is still raw, wild, and compelling. The seemingly infinite, large-scale topography between the Andes and the Atlantic rolls to meet the distant horizon. The truckloads of cordwood on the roads or stacked in towering rows around every home and business attest to an economy closely tied to firewood as currency. The more refined conveniences of heating oil and paved interstate highways haven't arrived yet. Massive ganglia of knotted phone wires dangle from poles above the street corners. Tiny two- or three-room cement block homes with tin roofs pack the hillsides. Friendly street dogs wander in packs or sleep in the shade of storefronts, occasionally bursting into territorial rumbles. No one speaks English.

The wind still blows across the pampas, the sun still shines, and many of the rivers of Patagonia and the Andes that spawn them are, for now, still wild and free.

The Mountain Will Set You Free

Skiing is often the topic of our family's conversation and Christmas lists in our house invariably include ski items. As a family, we plan and meet at a ski area at least once a winter for at least a weekend. Also as a family, we have traveled together to, or met at, Tuckerman's Ravine in the White Mountains, for nearly 20 years. Before the children were old enough to hike or ski it, the parents did, going 20 years farther back. When there's snow at home, we build and launch from backyard jumps. We've skied western states, Canada, Europe, and New England.

However, skiing is not convenient, and sometimes it's downright inconvenient. We remember the night one winter, driving to Vermont, when, on the interstate, the road was so icy that a fire truck spun out of control and smacked the rear corner of our van. We sought refuge at a motel for the night. Continuing into Vermont the next morning, we lost friction with the curvy state highway and slammed the right front corner of the van into the guardrail. We had to cinch the bumper to the grille with my belt, but we continued on. When we creaked into the parking lot of the inn, our friends, after greeting us, glanced at the van and said, "Would you like to tell us about your drive?"

So why do we do it? The obvious reasons of course: family

time, playing together outdoors, joy in the winter. But another, important reason is that skiing creates connection with the natural world through grace. Carving down a mountain engages both gravity and lift and overcomes the resistance we're used to while walking or running. And it is resistance that disallows grace: grace in the wind weaving through the trees, grace in the clouds crossing the sky, grace in water flowing downstream. At your best, you emulate these elements, tracing the contour of the mountain as you descend. Skiing is, literally and figuratively, both liberating from the bonds of earth and grounding at the same time.

A skier expresses herself through the edges of her skis and, in fact, "on the edge" is where she wants to be. The "edge" is the balance point between leaving earth and returning to it, the state of being weightless, and it lasts only a moment. But these moments are repeated with every well–carved turn, and in lilting, lifting succession, the skier tuned to the earth under her feet achieves a rhythm from the tension and release akin to that of a powerful symphony. As a ski trail can be considered a path, she defines herself through the expression of her turns on the path.

With the advent of parabolic, or shaped, skis, skiing has gone from two–dimensional to three–dimensional. The wider tips and tails and pronounced side cut of these newer skis demand a different technique. The goal is no longer to keep the skis together, parallel style, and to swish from side to side while shifting body weight. What straight–ski parallel aimed for, sliding *down* the mountain, has become carving *into* the mountain, as the skier is now required to lean the skis on edge and allow them to initiate the turn. As the angle of the edge increases, the radius of the turn tightens, until the skier transfers weight to the opposite edge and the sequence repeats.

We call this "fun" for a good reason. We feel unbridled joy

when we place ourselves in the background and find connection, unity, and harmony. When we link these three sensations in rhythmic turns, we mimic the cadences found in all of nature: the tides, the seasons, the sunrise and sunset. Just as an accomplished guitarist no longer looks at her fingers, a skier in rhythmic descent lengthens her line of sight to the slope far below. Without looking at her feet, her awareness of what they, and she, are doing grows. This increasing distance of perspective allows a larger view, and an expanded sense of place develops, and sometimes with that perception a strong attachment. As the skier responds in harmony to the mountain moving beneath her, she feels she is right where she should be: home on earth. She unites the horizon (the x axis) with the plumb line of the mountain (the y axis) and creates a floating sense of swooping, especially in the trail–wide turns, as she inscribes linked parabolas in snow. It is, when fully achieved, an elegant equation, filled with grace.

The Boy and the Beaver

April 2015

This morning I hurried out the door by 8:00 for my walk, trying to beat the predicted heavy rain. It was cloudy and getting darker, but I thought I had a chance. My goal was a fishing spot on the river that was a mile beyond the still-locked vehicle gate. I wanted to see if the recent high water had dropped enough at this pool to offer some promise of trout. Someone may have walked from the gate to fish it, but that possibility was unlikely. And the pool had not been fished all winter, raising my anticipation. I was nearing my spot when something moving in the river caught my eye. At first I thought it was a muskrat, but as it swam around, giving me a better view, I realized it was a young beaver. In over 30 years of fishing this river, I've seen only four beavers, so I was riveted on the beaver when a boy casting a fly rod waded into the river just downstream. I was again surprised, because seeing kids fishing the river is just as rare as seeing beavers in it. He waved to me. I waved back, and he said, "Look at that beaver. He's scary."

"It's nice to watch him," I replied. The boy waded out and approached me. I said, "It's pretty rare to see a beaver in the wild."

"Yeah," he said.

"How's the fishing?" I asked. "Catch anything?"

"Not yet," he said.

"Are you on vacation from school?" I asked, this being a school day.

"I don't live here. I'm from Maine, and we're out of school up there. We used to live here ten years ago." He was tall, probably in middle school, with short hair and a slight scar near his cheek. He wore a blue sweatshirt, hip waders, and wading boots and carried two rods, a spinning rod and a fly rod.

"Where in Maine do you live?" I asked.

"Near Bangor. That's the town most people know nearby. We actually live in Dexter."

"How's the fishing up there?" I asked.

"It's okay," he said, "but there's only brook trout about this big," he said, spreading his index fingers about seven inches apart. "There's no rainbows or browns." Then he added, with some excitement, "I caught a sixteen-inch rainbow in this pool two years ago," pointing to the hole in front of us.

"That's a big trout. Where have you tried so far?" I asked.

"I started at the hanging bridge and worked my way up." The bridge he referred to was another mile downriver from where we stood, and the closed vehicle gate, the only way in, was another mile upstream. If he'd been dropped off at the gate, he'd walked at least three miles by himself along a river with no vehicle access. There'd been no cars in the parking lot or any other hikers on my walk in. It was only 8:30 on a cloudy Monday morning.

"I'm impressed," I said. "That's a long way by yourself."

"I don't mind. It doesn't bother me," he said, a bit uncomfortably.

Right away, I felt bad for this boy. I was reading into the situation, but where was his dad or his uncle or his friend to keep him company and to watch out for him?

"Have you tried the pool just below here where the rapids

run out? I've caught some trout there and was just on my way to see how high the water level is." I pointed downstream.

"I saw that," he said, "but I didn't try it. A worm might be the right thing," he said as he pulled one from his Styrofoam cup and threaded it onto the hook on his spinning line.

We wove our way through 30 yards of brush and emerged at the edge of the pool, where the riffles came in.

"Sometimes I catch them up there," I said, pointing to the shallow white water. "But usually, I do better in the slower water of the pool itself. I went out yesterday, and the two fish I caught were in slow water."

"Oh, you fish too?"

"Yes, but yesterday was my first time out. The river's been too high and the water too cold."

He was standing at the pool's edge, ready to cast, and, not wanting to make him uncomfortable, I figured it was time to leave.

"Well, good luck," I said. "I hope there are trout there for you."

"So long," he said. "And thanks."

"Good luck," I said again, nodding toward him. Then I turned and made my way back out to the road.

As I walked, I considered both of these rare encounters. The young beaver and the young boy, each alone, had both been exploring territory, the animal seeking a home site, and the boy seeking a connection with a fish and thereby sketching a nascent connection with himself. Within each of these paths was the seed of what would shape their lives.

For the boy, finding that connection with the natural world, often intuitively at first, and pursuing it with the guidance of experience and knowledge, will help guide his growth.

For the beaver, life in water somewhere is certain, and his

search here for a home is the beginning of what, for beavers, becomes a series of home sites over the course of their lives. The boy, if he develops an attachment to wild things, can carry that bond inside himself where it may play a role in where he settles or what he pursues for a career. Both will be better off for the bond. As Mary Oliver writes, "Attention is the beginning of devotion."

Here were two rare beings, a working beaver in the wild and a young boy, fishing solo, far from home. I was suddenly both melancholic for the days when these sights were more common and deeply grateful that the river, wild and alive, still offered the boy and the beaver the opportunity to pursue their direction, each according to his nature.

Remembering Not to Forget

May 2015

Early one morning along the river I frequent, I found what old-timers call "river pink." It's a wild azalea, once more common, and I recalled the last time I saw one, on a different river, 20 years ago. It was so memorable I can still take you to the exact spot where I saw it. It resembles the domestic variety, with two notable exceptions. It grows from a single branch, with sparse foliage, unlike its hedgelike counterpart, and its fragrance is much deeper—deep enough to prompt distant memories, some of them quite clear, some now faint with the passing years, of a time when there were so many wild azaleas that there was reason for folks to coin a common name for them.

John Waldman's recent book, *Running Silver*, points to this loss, not of "river pink" but of Atlantic rivers themselves and their great fish migrations. We too, he reminds us, once had a Serengeti in our backyard. This loss of an unimaginable biological abundance, he contends, is also a loss of incalculable spiritual magnitude.

Although we prosper today in ways unknowable to a few generations ago, we have created a world in which we have impoverished our spirit. Many of us, blinded by our technological advances, haven't even noticed what we've lost. But some of us suspect there's a void in our being, an emptiness that no amount of technology can fill. We sense it with the silent falling of snow, the thundering power of a waterfall, or the crash of ocean surf. And we feel it as well with the vast migrations of earth's creatures.

A new branch of science, called historical ecology, gives us information about our sense of loss. Waldman, through his review of extensive historical documents, scientific records, and literature, gives us a clear picture of how rich our riparian environment was in our recent past. The plenitude in Atlantic rivers not long ago was astonishing. The author cites records from the late 1700s and early 1800s that show four men landing 6,400 shad in one day and 1,000 striped bass taken from a single trap during one tide. On the Susquehanna River in 1827, it took 100 wagons and carts three and a half days to empty one seine net. This single catch was estimated to have landed 15 million shad and river herring.

With the advent of the Industrial Revolution, milldams started going up—65,000 of them by 1840. Today, there are more than 80,000 that are six feet or higher. The resultant decline of migratory fish was horrific. By 2007 relative abundances dropped more than 98 percent for 35 species. These are the "ghost species," either human, plant, animal, or insect. We know they were present in great numbers not long ago, but our memory and their numbers fade to where their remnants no longer even register in our consciousness. It's this "forgetting to remember" that shapes our perception of the disappearance of our environment, to the point where we no longer notice that major portions of it are gone. And for each portion we lose of our environment, we lose a portion of ourselves. Waldman reminds us to improve our future by first remembering our past.

Most of us are familiar with the extinction of the passenger pigeon, the near extinction of the buffalo, and the current failure of ocean fisheries. We see such absence in the global collapse of the bee and amphibian populations, the slaughter of elephants for ivory or rhinoceros for horn, the plummeting populations of songbirds worldwide.

But it's not just in the natural world that we witness loss, but in the world of human history as well. Much of the world, even in Russia, has forgotten the deaths of over 1,500,000 prisoners in the Gulag labor camps as the history of Stalin's dictatorship has been rewritten as a period of "stability" in Russia. Turks killed the same number of Armenians during World War I, but that history has been consistently obliterated by the Turkish refusal to acknowledge the genocide. White people in the Western hemisphere have largely forgotten the 145,000,000 Native Americans killed in the 200 years after Columbus arrived.

The memory of these events fades with the passing of each generation, but their cumulative disappearance lands quickly. Suddenly we wake to a world of greatly diminished variety, strength, and beauty. The color in the world has faded to shades of gray.

Here in New England the loss of the great fish migrations produces an equal loss of wonder at the magic of life in all its forms. We have robbed from our own being the spiritual connection that sustains it.

It is not often that a book on a scientific event is also a treatise on a balanced way to live, but John Waldman has given us just that.

Why I Fish

June 2015

I caught four beautiful wild trout this morning right after breakfast, and the fact that I am able to do so fills me with an appreciation for all life like no other experience. The expression among fly fisherman that "the tug is the drug" helps describe the experience but doesn't encompass all of it by far. A wriggling or yanking trout on a fly rod connects me immediately in a viscerally tactile way to nature and specifically to the nature of a fresh water current, and hence to the earth's water cycle itself.

When I stand in a river I'm standing in the bloodstream of the earth, and it quickens my own. All at once I feel the pull of the current, smell the biota alive inside it, see the sweep of its curvature, hear the headlong descent, taste the sum of its watershed in a cupped hand.

Like no other pattern, the water cycle, through its movement in a river, touches us with the shifting, sparkling glimmer of the sun's reflection and most strongly in the pulse we feel in the press of water's surging current. There is an urgency in the river's flow, an expression of the destiny of the living world which the fish amplifies.

Landing a trout, the moment I've striven so hard to achieve, only lasts just that as I hurry to unhook the fish and return it to the river. I cannot keep the experience any longer than it takes to release the fish, during which I'm clutching at the fleeting visions of their beauty. Seeing trout face–to–face ignites my sense of wonder, a gift only possible when I practice my skill well. It comes as a treasure, suddenly revealing itself, as, upon reflection, an insightful realization might unexpectedly surface as epiphany.

Monet once remarked about fishing that "it was all very fine, but it leads nowhere." In fishing, I am angling for more than trout. In the water temperature, the strength of the current, the wind, the angle of the light and the shadow, the insect activity, and an infinity of other aspects, I am gauging my level of observation. I am also testing my openness to seeing what is noticeable, which makes me see something I wasn't noticing, which makes me see something that I now know must be there, but isn't visible.

I seek only to be awake.

Pruning Season

March 2020

It's been three years since I began restoring the old apple trees in our backyard. I neglected them for 20 years, during which time they became thick with overgrowth, too crowded with foliage to produce many blossoms but still providing some fruit, every other year. The second owner of our house planted them about 60 years ago, and their trunks are now 12–14 inches in diameter, about the same size they were when we moved in those two decades ago. They are standard trees, which is what was planted before dwarf and semi–dwarf trees were cultivated, so they can grow over 20 feet tall, and some of them have.

When bringing apple trees back to productive health the rule is not to remove more than a third of the tree in a year, so it takes at least three years if you do it right.

Each year, pruning those 10 trees took about six weeks, starting in late January, working on days when the afternoon temperatures reached into the forties. The low sun then is right in my eyes, so I work from a stepladder or extension ladder with my back to the sun, so I can see what I'm doing. I can work in the cold for only an hour or two at a time, on windless days without rain, and the weather in January provides but a few of these days a week. When I finish, in mid–March, the sun is higher and the temperatures reach near 60. Over that time, I've watched the buds slowly grow to the point where they become my calendar, urging me to finish before the tree awakens from dormancy.

The crowns of some of the trees extend over 30 feet in diameter, so there are hundreds of branches. Each one must be pruned, either removing growth for health or trimming it for guidance. The first tree is the largest. It took me six days, one branch at a time, to prune.

At the end, three mounds of cuttings, each the size of a large sedan, sit in the brush off the yard. They rot quickly, so next January the piles will be half their current size, on their way to becoming soil for new growth.

The work swings between drudgery, when it seems as though there is no progress for days and I look at all I've yet to do, and satisfaction, when the sculpted tree emerges from its former tangle, branches now massaged in sun and gentle breeze, limbs spreading open to the sky, welcoming their liberation.

I just finished my third year, and the trees are healthier, though not perfect. Of course, I'm not just working on the tree. This is an interactive process, with the tree working on me, too, requiring that I decide what to nurture, not just in the tree, but also in myself—what to keep, not only among the branches, but also among my traits, what to remove, not just from the limbs, but from my mindset, performing all with the goal of healthy life. There are questions to answer for each decision.

Is the branch growing up and out rather than inward and down? (Am I growing up and out, from self to other?) Is the angle of the branch off the limb the proper 45 degrees to support the weight of fruit? (Am I facing the right way to receive life's suggestion?) Is there enough space between branches to allow air to circulate and sun to shine through? (Have I spread myself too thinly, accomplishing little, or too densely, losing sight?)

As within the trees over the past three years, the answers are not yet fully formed within me. And also, like tree pruning, the psychological process is arduous and takes time. But it's work well rewarded, and I welcome the reminder that, just as the tree needs restraint and consideration to avoid dissipation, so do I.

Part Three
My Life

Tuckerman's

July 1999

"I made the reservation," I said, surprised at how easily the lie rolled out.

"Oh good," she said. "The Joe Dodge Lodge is a comfy place to stay."

Now, lying to my wife was risky and, to be honest, a first, but it wasn't as risky as what I was going to try to do. But because it was a first, it showed how desperate I was to prove something to myself by placing my status as a husband, father, and midlife breadwinner on the line. I should have recognized this as a telltale sign of a crisis, but I suppose that's a criterion for qualification as a crisis: the participant is blind to the signs until, of course, it's too late. The lodge had actually not been taking reservations, so I was counting on there being room. See what I mean about being late?

I was headed for Tuckerman's Ravine, the origin of extreme skiing, and the site of a famous race called the Inferno. First, there was the nearly six–hour drive, then an hour and a half hike carrying skis, boots, poles, and lunch to the shelter, where you can gobble a snack and don another layer. Another half–hour hike gets you into the ravine. Then you have to climb the 30 or 40 minutes to the top of the headwall. But difficulty of access is not what stands out. What distinguishes the ravine is the gradient. The exhibit in the lodge describes the pitch as more than twice what it takes to be designated as a double black diamond trail at a lift–serviced area.

However, in the 25 years since I'd last done it, I had mercifully forgotten these facts and was proceeding as if it was all just last week and I wasn't really 48 years old. Selective memory can be a blessing.

At 3:00 in the morning, before getting in the car, I gazed at the night sky, reading the stars for some omen of my trip. Finding the Big Dipper and Polaris was easy, and I took that fact, plus the fact that those stars were beaming, as portents of a successful pilgrimage. Through the darkness, I followed them north. They even shone through the glare of city streetlights, pooling on naked highways, until the rising sun claimed their light.

Nearing Gorham, New Hampshire, the snow–laden peaks of the Presidential Range mirrored the cobalt–blue April sky. When I pulled into the lodge parking lot six hours after starting, I realized that the thermos of tea, the sack of sandwiches, and the box of tapes were all untouched.

I ate a quick breakfast and changed clothes. With my skis holstered firmly on my pack, their tips bound with a bungee cord, my feet found the snow–covered trail. Despite the 25–year hiatus, the path was familiar, as our driveway is when coming home from work. Sunlight poured through the bare April trees in pellucid waves of brilliance. The mottled forest floor lay in alternating patches of snow and matted leaves, a brown–and–white quilt. But the skyline view dominated.

Pure white cones, tied between with ridges, rose over me. A chorus of mountains, their folds enveloping valleys and deep cuts, complemented the azure sky in which they stood.

Fifteen minutes into the hike, I removed my pullover and

vest. An hour later, at Hojo's, the shelter and start for the ravine hike, I quickly put them back on, and my hat and gloves besides. Here there was wind, and lots of it. Perhaps three dozen skiers sought protection from it, huddled against the shelter wall or one of the plywood windbreaks. Here also was the first full view of Tuckerman's Ravine.

A cirque of considerable proportions anywhere, but even more impressive in the East, it bears features named by and for the skiers who have come over the years. Hillman's Highway is the predominant cut on the south side. A few skiers dotted its slope. The term "highway" is a sarcastic moniker; the slit is perhaps five or six ski lengths wide and, at 45 degrees, it is a challenging exercise in high–angle turns. Other "trails" drape both sides of the ravine and are similar in line and degree: The Lip, The Gully, The Chute, and The Cut. What filled most of the view in front of me was the seemingly vertical rise from the ravine floor to the horizon, known as the Headwall. The skiers climbing on it were mere specks on a vast white background. With a half–hour's hike, I was at the bottom of it, leaving my pack at the collection of boulders known as Lunch Rocks.

Two lines of climbers were beginning the ascent up The Lip, and I chose the one on the right. Even though I began to kick steps into the slope almost immediately, the angle didn't get my attention until I could no longer shoulder my skis perpendicular to my body, tails in front of me. They began to spear the slope even when I stood up and were throwing off my balance. So I swung the tails out to the right, my skis touching both shoulders, and climbed in a three–point stance, with my left hand holding me into the now even steeper slope. I would try to make 30 steps like that and then rest. Every so often, a kicked step would collapse, and I'd waver backward, fluttering my free arm to catch my balance. Once, a step caved right into a hole, and my left leg went in up to my hip. A fellow climber, a few feet to my left in the other path, chuckled nervously and asked, "Did you fall into a crevasse there?" As I slowly pulled my foot out, careful not to lose my balance, and peered into the black hole below I said, "Yes, as a matter of fact, I did."

Shortly above, my path angled left and converged with the one used by more climbers. The steps had been kicked deeper with combined traffic and I was relieved by the extra margin of comfort. Another 20 steps and I was over the lip and into the strong wind coming down off the summit. The slope lessened to where I could walk upright comfortably, and I stopped to put on my hat and look around.

I could see the antennae on the summit station, although the station itself was blocked from view by a ridge to my right. Turning around, the sight back down the headwall caught my breath. Dropping from sight right below the lip, the slope did not appear again until far below, where people looked like ants. For the first time, I thought about walking back down. Then I realized that the slope was too steep to walk down except in the carved out snow steps. With the steps filled with people coming up, walking down was not an option. I imagined the headline, MIDDLE–AGED MALE RESCUED AFTER CHOKING ON HEADWALL, and the humiliation of that real possibility made me realize there was no turning back. I was going to have to do this, or look foolish trying. So much for the wisdom of the middle years.

I walked up about 30 yards, where a half–dozen skiers were putting on their skis. The spot was far enough from the lip to provide room for a few warm–up turns before the moment of truth. I watched as they pushed off, alert to the way they handled it, and when it was my turn, I followed.

"Followed" is actually the wrong word, because it implies

being led. When I set out I was not being led by anything except a riveting focus on my own situation. Skiing near–vertical terrain will do that to you.

The drop came before I was ready for it. The pitch was so steep that out of fear of falling I cut across the slope and gained too much speed to make a turn and skimmed along an exposed ledge to a rock wall, fortunately stopping in time, but in a fix nonetheless. I was facing the wall without room to turn around. One wobble and I would fall off. I had to turn around, and my solution seemed simple: step out of my skis, turn them around, and step back into them. But I had forgotten that simple doesn't mean easy, and I was reminded of that truth the hard way. To complete my about–face (and to save some face, for I knew I was being watched closely now by the spectators below and was imagining their conversation: "Who's the guy in trouble up there?") took the next 10 minutes, which seemed like an hour, during which I soaked myself with tension–induced sweat. When I finally stood up facing the right direction, I was exhausted, and I still hadn't come to the steep part, the lip. Doing great so far.

I didn't have a plan. My goal was simply to tape over the memory of years prior, when, skiing with my wife, she had carved her way to the bottom in beautiful turns and I had traversed, too afraid to make a turn in the fall line. I'd always felt as though I could have done better, and that meant overcoming my fear and committing to turns high on the headwall, where the angle is most intimidating.

The question of whether I could do that stuck in my mind as I pushed off; it got louder as my speed increased. My response was to veer off the fall line into a traverse, buying time before I had to initiate the turns that would prove I could do it. But it was only a delaying tactic, and I knew that. Within a few seconds I knew that any more traversing and I would remove my chance to vindicate myself. I was running out of slope quickly.

With all the commitment I could muster, I threw myself into my best imitation of a steep turn. It wasn't stylish, but it was functional and I stayed upright. "Do it again," I thought, "now, before it's too late." And I did. And with a few more quick twists I was at the bottom, gliding for Lunch Rocks.

While I chomped some gorp at the Rocks, I watched other skiers descend and reviewed my performance, debating what to do next. I'd made it down without humiliating myself completely, which in itself was an achievement of sorts. Yet I also knew that I'd avoided turning down the pitch at first, and I wasn't satisfied.

Inside myself, I already knew what I was going to have to do, and many of the other skiers, with their rhythmically symmetric turns high on the wall, only confirmed it. A bright orange parka above the lip caught my eye. I watched as the skier glided to the center of the headwall, where there was a narrow drop between two ridges of rock known as The Chute. It was trackless, and for a good reason. It was as steep as any part of the headwall but only two ski lengths wide. In the group where I was sitting all eyes were on this guy. The skier came slowly over the top and proceeded to make tight turns the length of the chute, going right to the rock wall on each side before carving back. It was a pleasure to watch, and I knew that that particular run would have to wait until I knew I could turn the way he had.

There was also the guy who was telemarking his way straight down the fall line where I had wanted to go, throwing arcs of snow in perfect rhythm. His control was impeccable; his graceful motion a beauty to behold. I also couldn't help notice that all of these guys were younger than I was. In most cases, a lot younger. But, I reminded myself, I wasn't here to keep up with them; I was here to prove to myself I could ski the fall line.

There was still time in the afternoon. The weather was

holding, and the snow was prime. And, having done it once, even if not perfectly, gave me enough confidence to try to do it again. At the same time, I knew I wasn't going to have enough energy for a third time. However I felt about myself after this second try was going to be what I took home, and it would have to last until next year. I finished my lunch, shouldered my skis, and began the ascent for one final attempt.

This time there were fewer skiers going up. The steps had been well chiseled by now, and my progress was quicker. On my way up, I kept reminding myself that the first turn would have to come right away, before I gained so much speed that traversing would be the only choice. The immediacy of that first turn was the key. I envisioned myself making that turn, just over the lip, and reran this tape in my imagination as I chugged my way skyward. At the crest, I looked closely for markers that would tell me where I had to begin that critical first cut and picked as my marker the narrow slot between two outcrops of ledge. When I got to the top, I stepped into my skis, drew a beam on those two caps of rock, and pushed off.

I made a point of doing the warm-up turns as aggressively as possible to get me ready for the first big one between the rocks. They served their purpose. By the time I made it to the lip, I had a rhythm, and the big turn there came naturally as a part of it. Fully committed, I threw myself into that turn with my complete being. Way out over my skis, with the angle falling away, I planted my inside pole and jumped. Both skis lifted off. All I heard was the bellows of my breathing, all I saw was the slope in front of my ski tips, and all I felt was the recoil of my knees into my chest. But I was leaning too far forward, and the compression upon landing nearly threw me over. The need to make another turn right away forced me to stabilize and launch once more. This time my skis turned in mid-air and landed, with me above them.

Focusing on my rhythm and the energy needed to maintain it put my fear of the pitch just enough in the background, and I made tight turns again and again, all the way down. I cruised down to Lunch Rocks, glowing with the mastery of fear.

There were a couple of handsome women seated on a rock near my pack, and as I stepped out of my skis one said, "I watched you come down. You did a good job." Mustering all the modesty I could, I replied, "Thank you. I was certainly trying to."

As tired as I was, the ski from there down was a pure romp. I shot to the base of the bowl and stopped to take a last look at the headwall. The lavender light of afternoon was beginning to descend into the ravine; the sky was cloudless and promised another starlit night. The mountain had been good to me, and I had done all right for myself. I turned and pushed off, carving turns through the soundless forest, savoring the peace of demons at rest. Until next spring.

Subjective Hazards

January 2003

Subjective hazards

Hazards that a climber may bring into the mountains include ignorance, improper training, poor judgment, inadequate equipment, poor conditioning, along with such psychological traits as overconfidence, false pride, apprehension or fear.

Ronald C. Eng, ed., *Mountaineering, the Freedom of the Hills*

Even though I'd signed up with the Exum Guide Service to climb the Grand Teton, the highest mountain in the Teton Range, I canceled my trip with the service when my friend Jack suggested we climb it together. He and I and my wife, Monique, had come close to summiting it once before, 17 years earlier, but had been stormed off. I'd wanted to return all the years since, but the birth of two sons had kept me close to home.

The events of that first attempt stood out in memory. The three of us had hiked six hours from the valley floor, arriving in the afternoon at the anchored rope on a rock face just below the lower saddle at 11,600 feet, where we had a permit to camp. We were taking a break when we noticed a man plunge–stepping down the snow above us. He moved frantically, throwing himself down the slope, and it was obvious something was wrong. When he reached us, he stood close to me, sweat pouring off down his face, panting. His eyes were wide open, his voice shaking and too loud.

"My partner fell a long way, and I don't know where he is. When I call for him, he doesn't answer," he blurted out, staring at me.

Before I could reply, he said, "I've got to get to the ranger station and begin a rescue," then grabbed the fixed rope and dropped to the snow slope below, racing headlong to the valley.

Jack, Monique, and I stared at one other, speechless.

"He's in shock," Jack finally said, "and it doesn't look good for his partner."

"By the time he gets to the ranger station, it will be near dark. Will the rangers begin a rescue then?" Monique asked. "Or wait until the morning?"

"They'll start right away," Jack said. "The climbing rangers have to be certified to rescue in almost any conditions."

"I can't imagine hiking our last six hours in the dark, with rescue equipment," I said.

"And it looks like it will be in the rain," Jack said as clouds moved up the slope. "We'd better get going."

We hustled up the remaining slope to the lower saddle, found a tent site, and were in the middle of putting up the tent when the storm hit. Hail so large we had to don our climbing helmets showered from the clouds, along with pelting rain. With freezing hands we scrambled to erect the tent in the deluge, threw our packs inside it and then ourselves. We laid out our sleeping bags and got in them to warm up our hands enough to fix dinner. After dinner we laid rocks on top of our tent stakes to keep the tent from lifting off in the storm. Eventually, we fell into uneasy sleep with the wind and the rain lashing the tent walls.

We woke up in the middle of the night to a ranger at our tent door.

"Hey! We're looking for a climber who fell, and we could use some help. Can any of you climb five point six in the dark?" he shouted over the wind. The rangers had, indeed, hiked six hours from the ranger station *in the dark. In a storm.* And now they were about to search for, and hopefully rescue, a climber. This would be done *on pitches steep enough to require ropes*, also in the middle of the night, in a storm.

The three of us looked at one another in the beam from the ranger's flashlight, thinking. A climb with a rating of 5.6 is considered moderately difficult. But it's not a hike. It still requires a rope, carabiners, and pieces of protection attached to the rock to catch you when you fall. All of us had climbed routes of 5.6, but never in the dark, in a storm.

"No, I don't think so," Jack said. "We'd like to help however we can, but in these conditions, we might not be the help you could use."

"Thanks anyway," the ranger replied, closing the tent door. We heard his boots crunch away and then the voices of the other rangers as they moved off.

"I hope they find the climber in time," Monique said. "They've got a risky search ahead of them."

"Certainly less risky for them than for us, but I wish we could help them in some way," I said.

"Even still, they're doing it in the dark, in a storm, after hiking six hours," Monique said.

"Let's hope they're safe," Jack said.

We didn't sleep much.

We woke to thick fog, a steady rain, and rumbling thunder. Visibility was around 50 feet and getting worse. We were awake and dressed and ready to fix breakfast when we saw the ranger approaching.

"You're going to have to move your tent. We've got a chopper coming to pick up the body, and your tent site has the widest radius of clear ground. The pilot won't land, but he'll send a winch cable down."

"We'll do that right now," I replied.

"That would be good. He's due soon."

Monique and Jack and I began stuffing sleeping bags and mats away quickly and then scrambled to take the tent down. With the rain pushing us, we cleared the site fast, then moved our loaded packs away as well and stood back. The ranger was on his radio, directing the pilot down through an opening in the fog, and then we heard the hammer of the blades moving up slope from the valley. Within a few moments, the chopper was overhead, lowering the winch line. In the roar of the blades and whine of the engine, we had to brace ourselves in the prop wash and cover our ears. The ranger grabbed the winch hook, clipped in the body bag, and signaled to the pilot to lift the cargo. The bag rose to within 10 feet of the chopper's skids, and then the helicopter pivoted and peeled away down to the valley. The noise diminished, then trailed off, leaving us standing in the rain and fog.

I was wondering what we were going to do, and I knew Jack and Monique were questioning also. We heard voices, and then climbers became visible, headed down. We knew it was a guided party, because all of them had daypacks. The Exum Guide Service provides lodging in a small Quonset hut at the lower saddle, where the guides also cook meals and store ropes, climbing gear, and sleeping bags, so the clients don't have to carry anything heavy. We thought the guide would have a current weather report, so we hiked over to meet them.

"Are you headed down?" I asked the guide.

"Yeah," the guide replied. "The weather reports are calling for this storm to continue, with ground lightning also predicted. Some of the guides have already felt it. None of their parties are summiting. Everyone is headed down."

"Thanks. That's good enough for us," I replied.

"Be safe," he replied, as the group hiked off.

Monique spoke first. "I'm ready to call it. None of the guides are going up and we shouldn't either."

"Fine with me," I said. "How about you, Jack?"

"No question. Ground lightning, no visibility, rain and wind. Not today," he replied.

We hiked down in the rain, wrapped in the fog and our thoughts. We'd seen enough.

When our two sons were 7 and 9, Monique and I took them to the lower saddle. They loved the exposed nature of the spot, the world dropping away on two sides to the valley floor 4,000 feet below and also rising north and south to the summits of the Grand Teton and the Middle Teton, with the black stripe of its diabase dike running right down its flank. We spent a night there at the base of a rock wall hundreds of feet high and watched the stars shimmer.

To make that trip, Monique and I waited in an early morning line at the Jenny Lake Ranger Station to reserve a campsite at the lower saddle. And so it was that Jack and I were waiting at the same place, also early in the morning, some six years later.

The office didn't open until eight, but we were there before six, and there were two climbers ahead of us. Two more soon joined us, and in the two hours of sitting we all swapped plans and stories. Jack and I had planned to reserve for the following night and leave early the next morning, but we learned that there were sites open for this night, so we changed our minds. Rather than wait a whole day, we decided to leave as soon as we could get packed. We'd climbed Teewinot, a nearby peak, the day before, felt ready, and the weather forecast, while not perfect, predicted afternoon thunderstorms, standard fare for the Tetons. We made our reservations for that same night and the following one, when, hopefully, we would be returning from our successful ascent.

By the time we packed all of our gear and were leaving the trailhead at Lupine Meadows, it was 11:30, and we were facing 4,000 vertical feet under 40-pound loads during the heat of the day. I thought of what the ranger had said when handing us our permits: "Be sure to get an early start," and I cringed.

We leapfrogged other groups on the six-hour hike to the saddle, one of which was a group of four lead by an Exum guide. Glenn Exum pioneered the route named after him, the one we were attempting, and his service's guides were well respected. The Exum Ridge included two sections we wanted to climb—Wall Street, a ledge that ramped up to a very narrow point, and the Friction Pitch, which had few handholds or places to fasten ropes. When I saw the Exum group, I didn't feel worried about our late start. I should have.

When we reached the fixed rope below the lower saddle, it started to rain. The Exum group had caught us, and they were all donning rain gear. I hoped it was a passing shower and debated just forging ahead, but changed my mind when it started raining harder. The effort it took to unload my backpack, put on my rain shell, and repack my pack, all done in the rain, left me so tired I could barely haul myself up the fixed rope and hike to the lower saddle. An early start would have put us in our tent at the lower saddle by now, having enjoyed a relaxed dinner, with more time to scout the next day's route. Jack was feeling the day too, but we made a quick camp on the uphill side of a large boulder as the rain stopped.

We ate a dinner of rice, tuna and mushroom soup and just as we finished, rain started falling again, harder this time, pooling under our tent. It stopped within a half hour, and Jack and I lifted the tent off its site and rolled it onto its roof to dry out the soaked floor. We rearranged the ground tarp too, to better deflect the water. Satisfied with our improvements, we walked to the western side of the saddle to see what weather might be coming and to scout our route for the morning. We'd followed a trail to the lower saddle, but from here to the summit we'd have to find the Exum Ridge route through the upper mountain's vast and varied folds of rock. After consulting our guidebooks, the route still wasn't clear.

Hunting around for clues, we met a climber who'd just summited by the Exum Ridge route, and he described the way from the lower saddle to Wall Street, the first part of the Exum Ridge route. Pointing up at obvious features, he said, "First, you climb up that gully to the Needle, which is that first large tower in the gully. You have to climb around and above the Needle and then climb down to the right, going east, toward the couloir that will lead to the base of Wall Street, which is the prominent ledge that really begins the Exum Ridge route. The turn east toward Wall Street isn't visible from here, but if you miss it and keep going up the gully you'll end up at the upper saddle. That's the Owen–Spalding route."

I was still uncertain about what to look for and listened carefully when Jack asked a few more questions, hoping for clarity. Jack sounded as though he was getting the gist of the route, but my sense of it was that we were going to have to feel our way up, checking the guidebook often, and that the features would become clear the farther we went. One thing for sure was that we couldn't miss the turn east to Wall Street. Having this climber describe the route while looking at the gully and still not be clear about it was not what I was hoping for. If we'd started the climb earlier in the day, we'd have had more light to scout farther and improve our understanding.

When darkness fell, another storm came with it, this one with a generous complement of wind and hail. We lay down for a restless night's sleep, with the wind leaning the tent over, the rain flailing at every seam, and my mind full of questions about the weather tomorrow and if we could find the route.

The scene outside the tent in the morning was hopeful; there were clouds to the west but it wasn't raining and there was no wind. Looking up toward the upper saddle, we could see parties on the route. It was late, about 5:30, and they were way ahead of us. I wished we'd started earlier; I wanted to be where they were. We downed our oatmeal breakfast, shouldered our daypacks, and headed out.

The route led across the lower saddle until it evaporated into the slope leading to the upper saddle. Up in the gully, the route to the Needle wasn't clear. Once inside a crease on the side of a mountain this big, with rock walls on both sides, you can't see beyond the walls of the slot you're in and you can't tell how far up the slot you are, nor how far you have to go. This was my first lesson in scale and how the route description translates to the real mountain. I wasn't exactly passing with flying colors. I had no idea of where we should turn east and descend to the start of Wall Street. The route description's last phrase in this section had stated, "Or you can just climb up the gully."

Unfortunately, the gully was a slide of loose scree, the smaller stones that a mountain sheds as it grows. But lacking any other clear direction, that's where we went, headed for the turnoff to Wall Street and the Exum Ridge route. Climbing blind like this was unnerving, and my apprehension persisted. I was coming to grips with the idea that I wasn't going to know exactly where we were. But I began to have faith that the direction we were headed would eventually get us to the turn to Wall Street, even though it didn't follow the guidebook exactly. I also felt we were doing the climb the hard way. Climbing over the scree, which slid back under each foot, was exhausting. Progress was slow and laboring.

"Jack," I said, "I'm not comfortable with the thought of having to come down this later. I hope we can find another way down." He kept moving up the gully with a confidence that made me think he knew where the turnoff was.

I huffed and puffed with the increasing altitude, glad I'd left my heavy camera at the tent. As the morning passed we picked our way up, the sliding scree underfoot maddening and tiring. I frequently paused and looked intently for clear signs of where to turn down into the couloir leading to Wall Street. Nothing stood out. Often I thought we had missed the turn, and as the hours dragged on, I became convinced of it. We slogged on until I was numb; then we suddenly crested the slope.

I immediately knew where we were, a tremendous relief, even though it wasn't where we wanted to be. From all the route descriptions I'd studied and photos I'd seen, we were at the upper saddle, and there was a party right in front of us just setting out on what I knew had to be the Owen–Spalding route. "Great, we can follow them," I thought. But we'd missed our turnoff to the Exum Ridge route, hundreds of feet below us, and with it the thrills of Wall Street and the Friction Pitch. So much for route finding.

"Well, at least we know where we are," I said gladly.

"I wasn't looking forward to the Friction Pitch after the rain last night, anyway," said Jack.

It was fine with me too. We still had a chance to summit.

The upper saddle sits between the west face of the Grand

Teton and a lower peak called The Enclosure. The Owen–Spalding route led out a sidewalk–wide ledge that narrowed, providing harrowing exposure on the north side to the nothingness of open air hundreds of feet down. The view to the northwest was immense and, as we approached the roped–up party, the route clung to the face. As we caught up to them, one member decided she didn't want to go farther and was led off by a guide for a scramble up The Enclosure. Later on and higher up, we saw them picnicking on that summit far below us.

The slow movement of the large group gave us a chance to catch our breath and watch how the route went out onto the face. While we waited, we chatted with the last climber of the group, a woman who was one of the trip leaders for this company's trips. She hadn't climbed the Grand Teton before either. The lead climber was an Exum guide they had hired. Jack chatted comfortably with her. I listened mostly, and watched. Closely.

When our turn came, Jack led out onto the ledge and soon had run out much of the rope. He also placed a few widely spaced removable anchors in the rock through which the rope passes. This was our protection in case one of us fell. I fed him rope and watched him disappear around a corner. He'd been out of sight for a few minutes when I heard him yell, "On belay!" I yelled back, "Climbing!"

I climbed out onto the ledge, stopping to remove each anchor and stow it in my pack. According to the guidebook, the route led through something called the Belly Roll, described as a large, detached slab, which we were supposed to traverse by hand along its upper edge, and the Crawl, a low space, roofed with a large flat rock. I just crawled through most of it. Catching up with Jack, I said, "I'm going to need knee pads if the route's like this to the summit."

"The mountain wants us to remember our humility," he

joked back. "Do me good. Haven't been to church in a while."

We had successfully completed the first pitch. My spirits were soaring, the sun was shining, and the view was of a scale I'd never encountered before. The woman in front of us had said she thought there were eight roped–up pitches to the summit. This was going to be fun, after all.

Our guidebook described the next section as an easy chimney. Jack led, again placing widely spaced anchors, and when he neared the top yelled back down to me, "This is way easy, Hugh." And it was. The small streamlet of rainwater running down it gave me a rhythm: climb the chimney, retrieve the pieces (I even unstuck an anchor belonging to the party in front of us that they'd been unable to remove), and climb higher.

At the top, we could actually see where we had to go. The visual route replicated the guidebook: "Continue upward and traverse southeast to the base of another chimney." We did this. Near the base of this chimney was also the rappel down for both the Owen–Spalding and Exum Ridge routes. Climbers were both ascending the chimney, headed for the summit, and descending the rappel, on their way down. Both routes share most of the same descent route, using this rappel to safely get climbers off the top of the mountain quickly. With both routes in both directions sharing this same small area near the summit, traffic jammed.

Unfortunately, some weather moved in. The sun bowed out of the afternoon and a gray overcast started to thicken. I began to feel a sense of urgency. To be so close to the top but have to turn back because of weather was an unpleasant thought. *If we have to, okay. But please, not unless we have to.*

Two anchored rappel ropes crossed each other, and we got in the line going up and noted the protocol. Ascending climbers were politely asking for permission to cross a belayer's rope to his climber on rappel, or courteously edging past the belayer in the narrow space available. The descending climbers were lined up for their turn on the rappel, down off the mountain.

I don't remember if we belayed or not, but the climbing up the chimney looked straightforward; Jack squeezed up first and I followed. And then an odd thing happened. We lost sight of the party in front of us; somehow they'd gotten far enough ahead or had veered off. Another element came into play also, as a lowering ceiling brought fog and zero visibility. We were running out of time.

We traversed to the north over rubble-strewn slab, which looked most logical, and sure enough, in a little while we spotted a high point that seemed to be the summit. When we got there we met a guide and his couple coming up from the Exum Ridge route and he corrected us. "Follow me," he said in a Spanish accent. "I've been here many times." He led us farther to the north and to the true summit, which was now totally socked in. Facetiously, he pointed down into the fog and casually remarked, "Here's the lovely view of Amphitheatre Lake and over here is Surprise Lake." Pointing to the south, he continued, "And over here are the tremendous views of Mt. Owen and the Middle Teton." His humor was contagious, and our spirits lightened. His clients called him Rolando, and I asked him where he was from.

"Argentina," he said, and then got talking with Jack about a former roommate of Jack's, a well-known climber ostracized for his climbing practices. I listened and gnawed on a protein bar, which tasted like sawdust, and watched Rolando savor a homemade sandwich with lettuce, which I envied. He offered to take our summit photo, and then it was time to leave. It was now about 2:30, and all I could think about was how we were going to get down with so little visibility.

Rolando and his clients disappeared in the fog, and Jack and I scrambled back down to the chimney, where we roped up and descended. In our hurry, our rope became hopelessly tangled, kinked, and knotted in the process. Poor rope management costs time, which is a safety issue. Straightening it seemed like an eternity. While we worked furiously to unravel it and worried about getting caught in a storm, Jack snarled, "Never buy another rope from this company." When we finally got it coiled properly, we scurried down to the rappel, where there was still a bottleneck. The party in front of us, the one we'd lost, was there, with three others and their guides, waiting to rappel off, and it was beginning to rain. The sense of urgency was palpable, as guides scrambled to get their clients down. One guide suggested to us that we tie our ropes together to get us all off quickly, and we readily agreed. Jack clipped into the rappel and went off first, and as soon as he yelled, "Off belay!" I followed. Over the edge I dropped, in a controlled descent through 100 feet of free air, touching down on the scree–covered slope. We waited for the guide's clients and then the guide himself to descend, untied our ropes, coiled ours, and followed them down. While I hoped the light rain would stop or at least not intensify, we trudged down a clear path, the guide and his client outpacing us. I was gleeful we weren't descending in the scree of the gully but instead were on footing that didn't move. At one point, just before the guide left us behind, the path faded out and Jack mentioned that the descent might go off to the west. "Oh, you can go that way," the guide replied, "but the gully is poor." We knew exactly what he meant. Even though we soon lost sight of him and his clients, following their direction led us eventually to the lower saddle and our tent.

Marmots had broken in and eaten all the protein bars, but it was still a cozy place to be. After our meal, a hailstorm unleashed on us, but we were snug in our bags. Sleep came quickly.

Morning broke with clear weather. We took our time packing up, not wanting to leave this rare, high place and our new relationship with it. We watched a guided party go down, and a few minutes later a new one came up to take its place. We chatted with two guides we'd met earlier in the week. They'd climbed the Middle Teton and were headed up the Grand. Having finally been there, I felt proud to have an idea of what they were headed for. More than a few times in the course of stuffing bags and tents, I glanced back up at what we'd climbed.

"We did it, Jack," I said. "Thanks."

"Yes, we did, Hugh." And then we both shook on it.

Hiking down, I floated on a sea of contentment, with a deeper understanding of my subjective hazards. I'll start earlier next time. For sure.

Early Fishing

August 2004

As a kid, my favorite possession was my fishing rod. It was a gift to myself and was actually more of a survival tool, an instrument for self–expression, a key to another world, a peaceful world that I needed.

There were three parts: the rod, the reel, and the line. The rod couldn't be too long and needed to be balanced and to have an even flex throughout its arc, without any flat sections. I preferred a cork handle with a double ring reel seat. That way I could move the reel up and down the handle to suit my preferred balance.

The reel had to be an open–faced spinning reel; closed–faced reels were constrictive and prevented full expression of your casting precision. An adjustable drag was important, too.

The line had to be between four and six–pound test. Too heavy and it crimped your casting; too light and it snarled easily, nor would it allow for real hefty tugging when you got snagged.

The whole setup, known as "my rod," took a pounding on my handlebars as I biked to and from my spots on the river. The rod was something that gave me adventure, led me to other worlds, and let me forget my family life. I took care of it.

You got a new one only when the old one was broken

beyond repair. Such events usually (and all too frequently) occurred in the jaws of a waiting door, sometimes to a house or sometimes to a car, or they could even occur during the course of cross-country escapades by getting into just the wrong spot.

If it broke at the tip, the best repair was to remove the tiptop (the line guide at the top) and try to fit it onto the broken rod, discarding the piece of rod. If the rod shaft had too wide a diameter to fit the old tiptop onto it, you had to get a wider diameter tiptop and glue it onto the rod, making sure to line it up properly with the other guides. There was special glue for this, called guide cement, which came in a candle. It needed to be heated with a match and then was applied to the broken rod tip. The resulting rod was functional, but because it now had a section at the tip missing, it was shorter and stiffer. Feeling the action at the other end of the line was a bit trickier. But it sufficed until the day I'd saved enough and was able to buy a new rod.

Sometimes my brother and I fished where we weren't supposed to. The most troublesome worry that hung over my head was a "what if." What if we got caught and they took away my rod? That thought was powerful enough to ensure our use of the utmost stealth, always slipping into forbidden water during the predawn hours. This meant that we had to leave home early enough and either ride bikes or walk. Early enough was usually between 3:00 and 4:00 in the morning. An hour's travel would place us streamside in time to sneak in under the cover of darkness and be casting to waiting monsters as the sun was rising. Darkness was a cover for admission, but it brought its own problems.

First of these were dogs. Neighborhood dogs that wouldn't look twice at you riding by in the light of day would go berserk if they so much as suspected your presence during the night. The ensuing racket always brought with it the threat of discovery.

Then you either had to run (or ride) for it, or answer to some agitated adult about what you were doing out in the street at that hour of the morning. Needless to say, we did everything in our power, including riding well out of our way, to avoid houses where we knew alarm dogs lived. No talking when passing these houses, stay low, avoid any noises at all costs. Coast as much as you could.

Of course, we could never tell for sure where these dogs might be, as the cast of characters changed frequently. Consequently, we traveled the whole distance as quietly as our skills allowed in perpetual vigilance against detection.

Having to be ever so mindful of our noise level taught us what was possible in this regard and showed us the benefits it afforded. Because talking might trigger getting discovered, we each had to travel as if solo, using only visual cues or hand gestures to communicate. You were forced to attend to these hints and observe closely, all senses alert, scanning for potential trouble around each curve. We were also blessed with the sights of the hour: the nighttime sky ablaze with stars, and later the day creeping in on the rosy fingers of dawn. Often we'd catch nocturnal animals on the move: skunks, opossums, deer, or raccoons surprised by our sudden, silent appearance. These sights were part of the reward. You knew you were seeing things others, sleeping in their darkened houses, wouldn't.

To avoid the paved roads as much as possible, we took shortcuts through fields or over stone walls, hefting our bikes and rods like voyageurs making a portage. We came to know the topography of our town well and developed a dependable sense of direction. In our efforts to forge new routes, we didn't always know exactly where we'd come out. But we had a rough idea and were willing to give new directions a try, ready for what the land had to teach us, about the lay of the earth and about the contours of our character. We were proud knowing we could set out and return safely, usually with fish, without asking for parental help, which, of course, was out of the question. But it was precisely because we had to do it all ourselves that we developed self-reliance and problem-solving skills. If your bike broke down in the middle hours of the night or you gashed your shin on a rock in a stone wall, you were left to yourself to cope. These were our self-administered tests of survival, our invented rites of passage.

We didn't always fish on posted property, but even to fish open water you needed to arrive early if you wanted to be successful. Early morning fishing simply worked best. Once the sun shone directly on the water, the fishing fell off and it was time to head home.

Now, though, the tension of the night ride had evaporated with the morning mist. We were dealing with an awakened world and were just two boys on their bikes with their fishing rods. We'd arrive home before noon, tired but fulfilled, brimming with discoveries, banking new memories. It always seemed liked we'd already lived the day, which we had. Someone would ask, "How was the fishing?" And whether we'd caught anything or not, we'd always say, "Great." And it still is.

Three Guitar Lessons

August 2005

In the summer of 1974, I was 24 and living in Jackson, Wyoming, with my girlfriend, Chris. I'd gone west thinking that's where my direction lay and to work on the golf course north of town. At that time there was no supermarket in town, and many people drove over Teton Pass to Idaho Falls to shop, about 90 miles away, a trip we'd make every two weeks. Much of the grocery store was a warehouse where ranchers shopped for their crews. Fifty-pound bags of rice and five-gallon cans of fruit and vegetables filled the shelves. The carts were the kind you saw in lumberyards back east, and had roll bars. Register receipts often approached 1,000 dollars. We shopped in the section of the store for retail customers. After food shopping we'd tour downtown, and it was there that I discovered a guitar I began to desire.

There was no music store in Jackson, but the one in Idaho Falls was called The Melody Shop, a name befitting a small business with a limited selection. But this store was big, not because Idaho Falls was big, because it wasn't, but because it served as the only wide-selection music store in a hundred-mile radius.

The "shop" occupied three large floors of a three-story building, two stories higher than any other building in town.

Pianos filled the first floor; brass, woodwinds, and violins the second; and guitars, banjos, mandolins, Dobros, and ukuleles the third. I had a Yamaha guitar that I wanted to trade up from, believing that if I had a better guitar I would become a better player. Actually practicing didn't enter my thinking.

At the time, Martin, Gibson, and Guild were the hallowed names in acoustic guitars, and when I saw the used Gibson Hummingbird for sale I was magnetized. The large, cherry sunburst body, the elaborately painted pick guard with the engraved floating hummingbird, and the inlaid mother-of-pearl parallelograms in the neck dazzled me. I played the few chords I knew on it and was impressed by its rich bass notes and clear trebles. I didn't realize that the larger, fuller sound from this guitar was produced by its dreadnought size, which was to be a problem. But there was one other, much more important fact that I wasn't aware of either. I just knew it was the guitar for me.

And so, over the course of the summer, I saved for that Gibson and would visit The Melody Shop each time we went to Idaho Falls to see if it had been sold. I should have been clued in when, with successive visits, it still wasn't sold, and I was able to trade in my Yamaha, plus 90 dollars, and take the Hummingbird home. It was then that I discovered the cracked neck, a feature, I learned later, that erased any resale value.

I told myself the cracked neck didn't matter because now I'd become the player I wanted to be. I am amazed now, looking back, by the fact that I failed to see, or chose to ignore, signs that could have steered me toward a more successful path, but such thoughts didn't fit what I wanted to see. And I wonder not so much if I still do this but *how much* do I still do this? How much of what I experience as my awareness, view, or consciousness is really factual or is just me seeing my preferences? I am haunted by this question. But the painful lesson from buying this guitar foreshadowed the lesson I was to learn from simply keeping it.

My job at the golf course ended with cold weather, and my girlfriend, Chris, was ready to leave her job at the daycare center, so we decided to return to Vermont through Canada. In packing, we included the only two new items of note we'd acquired, the guitar and the $700 we'd saved, and one thing we'd brought with us, which actually belonged to Chris, a small leather pouch containing substances for entertainment, which she hid under the mattress.

I suggested that she throw those items out, as they were old and probably no longer potent, and we were, after all, about to cross an international border. She chose to keep them.

At the crossing, all went fine at first. The agent asked the usual questions about how long we intended to stay, the nature of our visit, and did we have any items to declare, and I was ready to pull away when the agent's next question sank my stomach: "Would you please step out of your vehicle?" Numbed with the shock of the question and trying to look as nonchalant as possible, we waited nearby while she searched the van. When she emerged a few minutes later holding up the pouch she said, "Which one of you does this belong to?"

Following a night that one of us spent in the Canadian jail and the other at a campground in Piegan, Montana, we reunited the following morning for our court appearance. The proceedings were quite simple. With neither of us admitting ownership, the court assumed we were both owners, fined us $600 and prohibited us from entering Canada. We'd have to return to Vermont through the States and the $100 we had left was just barely enough to get us there. We arrived in the Green Mountain state with only two things to show for our months in Jackson: our insolvency and the guitar. To address the former, I got a job; as for the latter, I slid the cased guitar under my bed, where it remained, a reminder of a broken dream, for three decades.

In those years, I got married (but not to Chris), earned a master's degree, taught English for 30 years, and raised two sons. The Hummingbird still lay under my bed three years ago in May, when an asbestos alert closed the school where I taught. I was home alone all day and still getting paid until we were called back. The lesson of having done nothing about learning to play my guitar, the one I'd taken such good care of for all those many years, landed hard. I opened the case and started to strum.

Within a year I was taking lessons. The following year I attended a weeklong guitar workshop with my sons, where I took courses in acoustic guitar, songwriting, music theory, and improvisation, which I loved. I practice nearly every day now for an hour. And although I'm still an intermediate player, I enjoy playing my guitar. For quite a while, the Hummingbird's large size was difficult to get used to, but eventually I did. And even though an appraiser at a large music chain desperate to make sales looked at its cracked (but now repaired) neck and told me he couldn't give me anything at all for it as a trade-in toward a new model, it's worth a lot to me. From time to time, I browse the catalogues for a new guitar and have even played a few at music stores. The electronics come built in on many models now, and those guitars play a lot easier than the old Gibson. And then I remember that the Hummingbird is a lot better guitar than I am a guitar player. It's waited this long for me to catch up, and I'd better get going.

Glory Days

August 2005

I do miss their simplicity. Two dozen kids, one unmowed field, one football, and a fall afternoon in New England. This was all before computers and soccer programs, when neighbors spent time with one another, and their kids were on their own to invent their own fun.

We kids would bicycle in from all over, some only a few minutes away, some a few miles. All sizes, from fourth grade up to ninth, were drawn like pilgrims to their shrine, the field on Curiosity Lane, a street of older houses that spread down the hill beyond the field. We'd float in, like the leaves drifting from the trees, full of color, headed for our proving ground.

When all had arrived, we'd divvy ourselves up into teams. We were mindful of the balance of talent and expressed any dissent freely. The negotiations were as important as the game that followed, and we all knew it. Especially sought after or listened to were the comments made during the choosing up of sides. Compliments about so–and–so's running ability or his passing or tackling skills were given sincerely, with frank appraisal, and taken seriously and kept in mind for the game later. During the game, you couldn't waste time figuring out who was good at what. The resultant teams were as fair as they could be, and the kids were happy with them.

In this manner, players developed their reputations for certain positions. These didn't bind us, however, and you could find yourself playing any position, depending on who and how many had shown up. Consequently, everyone got to know every position, more or less, and what they were required to do during each play.

Rules were always subject to events: how many showed up, how much afternoon light we had left, the balance of big kids to little kids. In addition to these factors, and the most important, was an active sense of self-control. We were playing tackle without equipment, and certain infractions were seriously frowned upon. Any unnecessary roughing was heavily penalized, and the peer pressure to keep the play clean was effective. We all knew there were no adults to fall back on in the event of injury. That's not to say that players didn't get hurt, but when they did, it was by accident, and the teams worked together to resolve the situation. Penalties were sometimes decided through discussion between the teams, but most of the time the prevailing ethic dictated that the team that committed the infraction simply accepted the penalty given them by the opposition. Fairness in meting out penalties was important, because the tables always turned.

Our playbook was skeletal, but it allowed us to imitate our heroes on the New York Giants. We'd call post patterns, down-and-outs, buttonhooks, and the last ditch effort, "Everybody go long." Running plays included single and double reverses, end-arounds, and quarterback sneaks. In the huddle, the play calling was more of a committee discussion than a decision made by just the quarterback. Because everyone had input, all were committed to the success of the play. We did all this in our best imitation of the Giants players we deified: Y. A. Tittle, Frank Gifford, Carol

Dale, Rosey Greer, Jim Katcavich, Sam Huff, and the only non–
Giant, Jim Brown of the Cleveland Browns. We'd seen Tittle throw
game–winning passes in snowstorms with the clock running out,
Gifford and Dale snag passes and evade tacklers for extra yardage,
and the defensive power of the Giants front four. And even though
he didn't play for them, Jim Brown was the true giant. He set the
yardage records every year, during the course of which he'd often
carry two or even three defenders downfield before
reinforcements arrived and he'd be tackled.

These men were rugged and played with injuries; so did we.
Bloody lips, twisted ankles, sprained thumbs didn't put us out. In
fact, if there was a measure by which we gauged ourselves, it
wasn't the amount of damage you could inflict, which was looked
down upon, or even your talent, but rather, the amount of hurt
you could endure and still play. In our game this was the great
equalizer, and all saw it as a goal we all had a shot at. We
recognized, in our own way, that some kids were more athletic
than others, and we honored that distinction. But we respected
those who swallowed their blood along with their spit, held back
their tears and stifled their cries, got up and kept playing. Such
honor could only be earned. It kept us all equal, and we strove for
it. The greatest compliment a teammate could utter and the one
that motivated us to a higher level was, "You can brave it." And
with a slap on the back, you'd return to the huddle, knowing that
it was only through the struggle that you could achieve the joy.

And it was the opportunities for joy that kept us coming
back. Within our world on that field, among our peers, with no
adults around, what we sometimes accomplished were feats of
Olympic proportions. As a fourth grader, to take down Charlie
Hulin, a ninth grader who played on the high school team, left you
fulfilled inside. His knee in your teeth was a small price to pay. To
deftly evade or fake all manner of defenders and still catch the

pass or gain ground running was sufficient reward for all the times you'd end up with your face in the dirt. To draw in the defenders as you waited to loft a well-timed pass, only launching at the last possible moment, or to block once, get up and block again were gifts you could only give yourself, and their glow lasted a long time.

Eventually, usually after the sun had fallen to the treetops, someone would say he had to go, and the rest of us would chime in and we'd all mount our bikes and head home in the long shadows. We never mentioned the score, win or lose. It didn't matter. What each of us had, pedaling home in the gathering darkness, were moments of brilliance crystallized in time and the promise that tomorrow we could strive for them again.

The Coyote

June 2009

In the early morning hours of October 17, 2006, while out running, I was attacked by a coyote. The animal control officer I was speaking to in the hospital officially listed it as an attack by an "animal," because I hadn't been able to tell much about it in the predawn darkness and could only guess its weight, but its identity was confirmed later. The officer arrived at the hospital within an hour of my admission, while I was getting stitched up, and his appearance so soon had surprised me. He introduced himself and said, "I'd like to talk to you about your event." He wore a neat green uniform with a gold badge pinned on his shirt pocket. He was friendly, but official. He was looking for facts.

"The hospital is required to report any animal bites to our office immediately," he said. "In fact, I've already been to the site you described to the intake nurse. I searched the woods in the area but didn't find anything. Would you mind telling me what happened?"

As I began, he took notes and stopped only when I did. The doctor was just pulling out the rabies syringe. I had 20 new stitches in my right wrist, knitted together in the shape of a Y.

"I'd like to have your clothing tested for rabies at the lab, and then I'll return them. Would that be okay?" he asked.

"Sure," I said. "How soon would it be safe for me to resume running that route?"

"I'd say you'd be okay in seven to ten days. That will give the animal a chance to move out of the area. Oh, and one more thing. I don't know how you want to handle this, but get ready for the press," he said.

"Oh, really?"

"Yes. Everyone's going to want this story."

By the time I got home, the answering machine was full of calls from newspapers and TV stations requesting interviews. My thoughts were with the coyote.

A death from rabies is like no other. Sometimes taking months, the virus slowly works its way toward the brain, where it causes acute encephalitis. This inflammation triggers intense pain and exceptionally aggressive behavior in animals. Medical sources cite that, in humans, symptoms include paranoia, terror, and hallucinations leading to delirium. But who is to say they do not also occur in animals? The very name of the disease, after all, comes from the Latin of the same, meaning "madness." This is what I imagined the coyote to be suffering, without a healthcare system ready to provide relief, but with, instead, a community ready to exact revenge. Two days later, the coyote staggered into a backyard nearby, where a caretaker bludgeoned it to death with a peavey. The autopsy confirmed the rabies. And the killing confirmed the revenge.

There was one reporter already in the driveway, and as we talked others arrived. The phone kept ringing with new requests. One TV crew appeared and shot the piece; another took its place. The crews wanted to see the stitches, hear the vicious growl, and picture the primal battle of man vs. animal. One had me stand outside, in the black, windy night, to film that way for heightened effect. These guys have a job to do, I told myself, and their audience deserves the story. I told them what I could remember of escape and failed tremendously at my 15 minutes of fame. By 10:00 p.m. the media had all left.

It wasn't until then that I had a chance to reflect on that morning's event. The clocks had just changed, and there was no starlight. It was overcast, before dawn and very dark, conditions I was used to. As an early morning runner, there are times of the year when you adjust to the dark and times when you adjust also to a profound silence. No birds are singing, there's no wind moving, and there's no traffic. What you become acutely conscious of is your own footfall and its rhythmic counterpoint, your breathing. And then your thoughts drift away as you let the forward movement take over.

I was coming down a hill on a dirt road when I heard a rustling on the opposite side. Still running, I turned at the waist, more out of curiosity than alarm, and the animal was on top of me, tearing at my raised wrists, shredding clothes and skin. My scream came from my ancestors, disembodied and haunting. I remember violent flurries of slashing and still more screaming. I remember thinking I had to stay on my feet and that I had to protect my face.

We broke off, and I ran a few steps when I heard scratching nails accelerating in the dirt behind me. I turned and took aim at a patch of blurry fur that looked like it might be his underside and kicked as hard as I could. The crack of connection inserted a pause, and I fled once more, running the last mile home, holding my breath to listen, and glancing over my shoulder into the blackness.

This is what I'd needed to tell the reporters, and more. I wanted to tell them that I was thankful, grateful even, for the experience the dying, raging coyote had given me. My wounds would heal, but when would my roar ever again fill the night? And when would I ever again feel so close to my life and to all life by fighting so hard for it?

Beyond the Buoys

July 2010

It is early July, and the setting, just–past solstice sun seems determined to brightly illuminate the world for a few last moments before its evening exit. The effect is magnified manyfold as the light ricochets off the lake's surface, throwing wave-rippled beams everywhere. Facing this radiance I am blinded. Turning around, I see the landscape behind me glowing.

The beach and the water inside the buoy line are filled with bathers: kids playing Marco Polo in the shallows, parents launching children from their clasped hands, bodies sprawled on towels or the grass or sitting at picnic tables. A trio of kids follows a young girl with a spinning rod as she casts to the sunfish in the weeds near shore. Two canoes glide farther out, along the far shore, where the day's closing ritual at the summer camp, a speaker-delivered bugle melody, is fading.

The lifeguard is off duty, and her chair lying on the beach is our cue. My wife and I, standing in knee-deep water, strap the Velcro to our ankles, to which the line to the foam noodle is attached, and don our goggles. I look down-lake to the farthest end, where the yellow–and–blue raft is anchored; that will be our turnaround. It is big enough to house a trampoline, the pontoon ring rising a yard off the water, but from here, it's a mere button, distinguishable only by its yellow and blue segments. To reach it swimming at my pace, a mix of crawl and breaststroke, will take half an hour. It's the first time this season I'm trying the full distance.

We swim out and over the buoy line, tugging our floats, and the familiarity of open-water swimming returns. The shores are now the boundaries, not the buoy line, and, as we swim out, even the closer shores are looking farther and farther away.

We are not new to lake swimming. Summers ago, we stayed at a hostel on a lake in the Canadian Rockies. Every morning, a pod of creatures would pass far off our dock, traversing the lake lengthwise. The lake was over a mile long, and it seemed an impossible endeavor for humans; consequently, we didn't see people. We saw seals perhaps, or dolphins, even though our minds rejected these as impossible in this mountain lake. But as we watched, those visions fell away until the only plausible one remaining was of humans, defying the rules of our perception. And for the first time, we saw what was actually there.

The strokes come easily, the clear water gliding smoothly over every pore, and the breathing assumes its metronomic rhythm. The cord to my float tugs at my ankle. No motorboats are permitted on this lake, so even though my profile is low, I'm not worried. My wife and her float are already far ahead, and when I pause to switch to the crawl, I pause long enough to find her on the waterline and I know she's looking back occasionally too. It's an unspoken agreement—neither of us willing to verbally probe the possibilities.

The pattern of inhalation, stroke, exhalation, stroke, assumes a dreamlike background of gurgling and surge upon which I glide. Turning my head up to breathe, I track the piercing glow of the sun. Below water, jade near the surface fades to the black of the depths. My internal compass is rusty, and although I try to stay on course for the raft, I instead zigzag my way with repeated corrections, while my wife, like a train, swims straight for the raft. She's even farther ahead now. But I am glad I'm not tiring, and am pleased with my steady, if wandering, progress. This is not a race, but rather a deliberate effort to avoid rushing, to avoid being distracted by life's endless stream of errands parading as urgencies or even emergencies. So much of what we do clutches at our being with a desperation that smothers it, and ourselves, in unconscious panic. Yet the moment is always there, waiting for us to slow down enough to see it.

With each turn at the forward crawl, I pull longer at it, trying to build my endurance. I am happily surprised when, all of a sudden, the raft looks much larger and I know I will reach it. With the closing distance, holding a straight line is easier, and I touch the raft to confirm this stage's completion. My wife and I bob on our foam noodles, chatting in hushed voices, prompted by the deep silence surrounding us. In this silence and in other respects, open-water swimming is akin to ascending a peak. With conscious exertion, both bring you to a remote location where a new perspective is enhanced by long views. These views, and the peaceful fulfillment that come with them, are rare enough that you find yourself wishing you could stay. But you can't.

There isn't a ripple, and shade is appearing on the shore where the sun is setting. After a few minutes of treading water in the weightlessness of extended immersion, we stroke again, this time for the beach.

On the return, I swim through pockets of water so warm that it's a relief to enter the cooler liquid on their farther side. Sporadically, there are also pockets of frigid water, which remind me of the springs far below, the only sources this lake has. And so, even in its uniformity of essence, the lake manifests its variety of expression.

I am able to maintain the crawl for longer stretches now, and the return trip seems to flow. Now lifting my head to breathe away from the sun, I'm even able to track straight for the buoys. It's been just over an hour, but I step onto the beach as with new legs that wobble with adjustment and suddenly remember a book I studied in college about one man's waterside life. Thoreau described a pond as "the earth's eye, looking into which the beholder measures the depth of his own nature." My look has been more of a glimpse today, but it has been enough, and heading for the car I am grateful.

A Death in the Fall

August 2020

I was standing up at the wheel of the tractor, scanning ahead for woodchuck burrows hidden in the tall grass of the rough and glancing back frequently and nervously to confirm the fact that the five gang mowers I was towing hadn't locked up. The late October sun, near setting, threw long shadows across the fairways. I was close to finishing, when I could unhook the mowers and head for the maintenance barn.

So I don't know how long the woman on the first green had been frantically waving her arms in my direction when I finally saw her. She jumped, ran toward me a few steps, and then, as if distraught with her choice, raced back to the green. I waved in return, turned off the engine, leapt off the tractor, and ran, my work boots pulling like tennis sneakers on the fairway. It was only after I came over the rise that I could see who she was and that her husband was lying on the green nearby. She stopped waving then and paced back and forth on the apron of the green, until I arrived, panting.

"Hugh, it's Harry. He just went down." Sunny's eyes brimmed, but her voice was steady. Her gray hair glistened in the low rays of the sun. I knelt at Harry's side, pulling up what I remembered of CPR, hoping I could do this right. He was lying on his back, with his face up. His chest was still and his eyes were closed. I propped his neck on my sweatshirt and began. I pinched his nose, tilted his head back to open his airway, took a deep breath, covered his mouth with mine and exhaled. I was relieved when his chest rose in response, and I found a rhythm that felt closest to my own. I added chest compressions, in what I hoped was the correct ratio to breaths. Then, suddenly, Harry's cheeks collapsed and my exhales were blocked. His false teeth had detached and were obstructing his airway. I swiped with a finger to remove them and continued. Without teeth providing structure for his mouth, however, keeping his airway open became difficult, and I had to shape his mouth with my hands while still holding his head at just the right angle.

Sunny sometimes watched for a while and sometimes looked away, sweeping the course for someone she could signal to for help. But being midweek in late October, and out of sight of the clubhouse as well, we were alone. The minutes passed, my back ached from kneeling, and I drifted to memories of Harry and Sunny.

Or I was about to when Sunny broke in. "Oh, let him go, Hugh. We've had a great life, and some our best times recently have been with you and Monique. She is such a treat, and a lighthearted Spanish tutor. Harry loved the lessons as much as I did, which was why he was always kidding around. He made them fun in his way, by being such a pest, as Monique did in hers. For him, making the daiquiris after the lesson was his way of continuing the party. She and he enjoyed the playfulness and we all benefitted."

While giving breaths I composed sentences and during compressions I spoke them.

"When I picked her up after the lessons, you were all so happy. She was bursting with what a great time it had been and told me all the details on the ride home. Her connection with you and Harry was very special in her heart. She thought you both knew how to live."

My legs quivered with fatigue and my hands shook with cold, but I couldn't quit until medical personnel took over. Finally, a pair of golfers came over the hill hitting toward our green, and Sunny waved her arms and approached them. Within moments, they were racing back toward the clubhouse and Sunny was walking back to Harry and me.

"He said he'd call the ambulance in Londonderry. It'll be about fifteen minutes."

We were both silent for a while, Sunny pacing and me bent over Harry trying to keep the correct rhythm. We were in shadow now, and the cold ground chilled my knees.

Trying to keep Sunny company, I said, "When Monique and I were restoring our house in South Derry, she repeated the story you'd told her about the time you and Harry were fixing up your place years ago, during the peak of the tourist boom."

Sunny talked as she walked, like an actress delivering a soliloquy.

"Harry would shout the measurement down to me and I'd saw it, careful to leave the pencil line, just as he taught me. Our teamwork improved as we went along, and pretty soon every board fit, and almost always the first time. At the end of each day, we'd pour a glass of wine and sip it by the fire. When I looked at what we'd built together, even many years later, I could recall the days and what we'd done, could see the boards, see Harry and myself, and sometimes even recall what we talked about. That's what they mean when they say you live every moment twice, once when it happens and again when you remember it."

"Only the memories change with time," I replied, "and are often improved by it."

"No doubt they change," she said. "Often toward what we'd prefer. Perhaps it's the mind's play to have positive recollections to center on, maybe even to convince ourselves that we've led a good life."

I considered this and said, "You and Harry led a good life together. And even given various definitions of what a good life is, your love for each other and for life, as well as so many other people's love for you is confirmation. What else gives a life meaning?"

"Loving the struggles as much as the successes," Sunny said. "How we handle the challenges and disappointments provides the depth that life needs to be rich and alive. Struggle keeps us awake. To embrace life requires embracing work."

I was thinking of the struggle Sunny would face with Harry gone and said so, before I considered how callous it might sound.

"Oh yes, I'll struggle. It's a big change after nearly fifty years of life together. But I am alive and part of my living is, thankfully, the life I had with Harry. The strengths from our time together are a source of meaning in my future."

"I'm glad you feel that way. Please remember that Monique and I will always be there for you."

"I hope you visit me in Florida, one of these winters."

The ambulance appeared at the top of the hill without sirens or lights, came down the fairway slope and pulled to a stop next to the three of us.

The EMT got out and asked, "How long have you been giving CPR?"

"About half an hour," I said.

"Has there been any response?"

"No."

"Okay. Thanks. I'll take over from here."

He pulled the shock paddle from the ambulance and

prepared Harry for the jolt. Three times we watched Harry's chest jump, and then, the EMT said, "There's nothing more we can do here, I'm afraid. We need to move him to the hospital."

"I'd like to follow you to the hospital," Sunny said. "Can you give me a lift to my car? It's in the parking lot."

"Sure," he replied.

We stepped back while the EMT and his partner lifted Harry onto the gurney and into the ambulance.

Before Sunny got in, she gave me a hug and said, "Thanks for everything."

The vehicle rolled up and over the hill, silhouetted by the setting sun, and was gone. I walked back along the fairway to the tractor and unhitched the five gang. The tractor started, and I returned it to the barn across the road from the clubhouse, slid the barn door closed, and clicked the padlock on the hasp. I heard voices coming from the bar in the clubhouse. In the truck's rearview mirror, small clouds of dust rose in the setting sunlight.

Part Four
Family

Four Tramps in Trout Time

July 1992

I am one of the four men on the trail headed for the backcountry. The one behind me is Thor, my father–in–law. Behind Thor, my brother Ben brings up the rear. Andrew, the youngest, is leading, and at a good pace. His gait seems hurried by doubts of his memory concerning the correct direction to take. He has been here before, but it's been years. He's the brother of the groom, to be married in a couple of days. We've all come long distances to attend the wedding: Thor from Norway, Andrew and Ben from the West Coast, myself from the East. It's partly the distance we've come and partly the terrain we're crossing that make this trek feel like a safari. We are trout fishing in the mystical land of Yellowstone.

It is hot and dry, the sun beating down from a big sky of mostly blue. A few cheery clouds move slowly across it. I am awed by sheer size, not so much of the mountains surrounding us as by the vast distances to them. We are afloat on a parched grassland in a sea of still air. After walking for over half an hour, I can still look back and see our car, small but distinct across the broad flat of tan sagebrush and cheat grass. A group of hikers and a string of packhorses plod in the far distance behind us.

Andrew stops to point out a Mormon cricket, an insect that

at first glance makes me think of an armadillo. If you picked it up, which is not something you contemplate, it would easily span the palm of your hand. It is a cricket of plague proportions. I remember from elementary school social studies how the Mormons had to survive attacks of crop-eating locusts, and this cricket comes to mind.

We crest a rise and arrive at a fork in the trail. While Ben and Thor catch up, Andrew gets his bearings. The left trail leads farther up the valley, the right one to the Lamar River. We debate as a group and then go right. Thor is 72 and we have been walking in direct sun for nearly an hour. There will be plenty of river to fish. From the ridge, we see a herd of bison in the distance. Charred stubs of brush are scattered throughout the sagebrush, evidence of the wildfires in 1988, three years ago. As we approach the river, small stands of aspen appear, settled in clefts where moisture collects. Even though the path doesn't take us through them, the sight of their shade is refreshing. Some of their trunks are blackened.

Quickly, sage becomes knee-high green grass, and we drop through a copse of aspen to the river. A hiker wearing a red-and-white baseball cap suddenly catches up to us. He is a young man, and I wonder how he covered so much ground so fast. As we exchange hellos, I look for his fishing rod. Not seeing one, I am relieved as he quickly heads upstream.

We rig our rods and split up, agreeing to leapfrog downstream. The river looks small, perhaps because its banks, needing to contain spring runoff, are so much larger than the band of water they now contain. Behind a tree-lined bank, the river glides over a riffle into a small pool. Being the last one to set up, I pass my friends as I walk downstream, looking for my starting point.

I gaze carefully and walk slowly, scanning for likely lies. The water that I think looks good is relative to the other water I've seen, so I pass a few stretches that seem as though they might hold fish until I get to a piece that jumps out at me. Part of the purpose of this reconnaissance walk is just to savor my surroundings. The terrain is so open that there doesn't seem to be anything I can't see. To the north I can see Andrew, way upstream, standing in the riffles, casting to the undercut bank. Stretching from either bank, beyond a thin fringe of foliage, are the sage flats, reaching to their end, where the pine and fir-covered mountain slopes rise. Downstream, the river sweeps in wide bends until its ribbon vanishes. From where I'm standing, Andrew's cowboy hat is his most prominent feature. I know from our conversation this morning that he is in transition from a software troubleshooting job at a large university to an as yet unknown occupation. He has applied to medical school. Other members of his family have described him as finding his way. As the older brother of the groom, who is settled into a doctoral program and getting married, I wonder if Andrew is feeling some pressure to establish his direction. What he's doing now is his answer.

What's caught my eye is a straight piece of water that lies well below Andrew. Along one side is a calm, deep channel against a steep, eroded bank. I stop at its head and put on my sunglasses to inspect it, grasshoppers clacking all around me. The sun is strong, although there are more clouds now. I decide to fish the run upstream, so I enter at the tail of the pool and, after a pause to settle in, begin casting upstream. It is important for me to begin gradually, building consistency and a sense of rhythm.

Not that experimentation or even radical departure from the norm is ruled out. These leaps or accidents, as the case may be, are as much a part of my exchange here as is my ritual. I am in hallowed country. I have come a long way, and it has been a long time since I've been here. At the end of the day I want to feel as though I've done it right.

So I build cast length gradually, slipping stripped line from my left hand to join its part looping overhead. With the increased casting length my focus becomes more concentrated, to the point where I'm intently following the course of the fly, despite the glare off the water. At the same time I'm increasingly aware of all that is going on around me.

What I'm aware of, besides the fact that some very hopeful lies haven't produced a single strike, is that the sky is filling with dark, rolling clouds. At the point where I have covered nearly every corner of the reach with the fly and am beginning to wonder where the fish are that must be here, a trout strikes, and after a sporting resistance, I land him. Immediately, I am reminded of the unique nature of this trout, the Yellowstone cutthroat. The yellow sides darken to a deep pink toward the gill plates, under which are the namesake gashes. I release him, wade out, and walk downstream.

I walk for a while without fishing, seeing nothing that hints at protection a fish would seek before a tuft of grass, the first feature I've seen that stands out from the cobble–strewn expanse, catches my attention. It's just a small bunch, barely hanging out over the water, but I cast to it anyway, more out of distraction than conviction, and am immediately awakened by a strike and, a short while later, the fish. What I had been seeking were the telltale grand features, like a prominent seam line in the current along an eddy. But those I'd missed were subtle: a narrow strip of shade along the bank, a barely perceptible swirl below a submerged rock. From then on, I cast to every little shrub or branch.

Working my way down, much more of the water now seems promising, as I arrive at what I immediately sense has to be "the place." A bend courses over a rounded rock bottom and glides into a pool deeper than the water I've seen for the past mile. Clusters of lush shrubbery line the far side, which rises steeply out of the river in gravel–bank fashion to a height above my head. More than halfway across is a large rock, mostly submerged, around which the current is evenly divided. The perfect lie.

I carefully walk to the tail of the pool, check the leader and the knot on the fly, and begin to cover the water upstream toward the rock. Working the line across and out in increasingly distant loops, I slowly close in on my target. Disbelief sets in, as cast after cast remains untouched. I've covered everything to the rock by now, yet nothing has happened. With nowhere else left to cast to, I cast even farther upstream, far beyond the rock where I felt so strongly a fish would lie. I'm at the furthest reach of my cast, and of my persistence, when the fly touches down and, after a drift of only about a foot, disappears almost inaudibly. The fish makes its size felt immediately, as wide bands of pink chrome flash beneath the surface. I gradually bring the fish to the net, where he measures over 20 inches. It is not just the largest cutthroat I've caught; it's the largest trout I've ever caught. If I were to keep a fish, this big one would seem to be the choice. Yet he seems the most venerable and, as such, still has things to teach. Upon release, he recovers slowly and resumes his position above the rock.

The rumbles in the sky become clashes as the now charcoal clouds stride with intent. Thor arrives upstream, wades to the middle of the fast water, and begins casting. He is not in waders, but is wet–wading in khaki slacks. He is tall, with flowing white hair, and the khakis and white shirt give him the appearance of a beachcomber, with only the straw hat missing. His nine–foot antique rod fits him comfortably, and he fishes in a way reminiscent of turn–of–the–century engravings, slowly and evenly turning the line over. He, too, is feeling his way again in once familiar territory.

A few casts later I'm rewarded with another fine trout, nearly as large as the first. While I land it, Ben arrives. He's fished above me, catching an occasional trout, and is impressed by the size of the cutthroat I'm releasing.

"Why don't you fish the rest of the pool, Ben? I'm ready for a break," I say.

"I think I'll just take you up on that," he replies.

Then I stand back to see what happens. As I watch him roll out casts in tight loops, in full control of his side of the equation, I remember the last time we fished together. Though only a couple of years before, it suddenly seems much longer, as the Ben I'm now witnessing seems so much different from the Ben I saw then. It's the point at which you realize you're not thinking of him as your little brother any more. And you realize that's because he isn't any more and maybe never was in the way you've always believed. And then I realize that Ben is not the one who's changing in front of my eyes. It's me. Ten years on opposite coasts has done this, and the reality of it lands firmly, with a decade's weight. The shock of it lies in my not acknowledging the change until now. I am afraid to consider what other sudden shifts in the fraternal fault line await my recognition. While troubling over why it's taken me so long to see this, I am returned to the river by a roll of nearby thunder.

I catch Ben glancing speculatively at the sky while trying to maintain control on a long line shooting overhead. It's a delicate balancing act he's performing out there, with an insistent cloud bank pressing a closing, and his skill is rewarded with a strike from the head of the pool.

With his rod arced, he looks at me, beaming, and as I return his broad smile, I realize my worry is gone.

The Mt. Shasta Climb

August 1995

"Ben, when I come out, I know we want to fish mostly, but I also want to try climbing Mt. Shasta and wonder if you'd be interested in joining me," I asked my brother. I didn't know if he would be, but my flight to California was a month out, and he'd need time to prepare if he was.

"Maybe," he replied. "The mountaineering shop in town rents the gear. But I'll need to get in shape by then. And it's been years since I've carried a pack, and I'm not sure my foot would hold up." Ben had suffered a terrible childhood accident with a lawn mower, in which he'd lost much of his right foot, and fitting that shoe had always been a problem. "How much do you know about the climb?" he asked.

"I bought the climbing guidebook and read it a couple of times. Avalanche Gulch is the easiest route, and the one most climbers use. We won't need ropes or protection, but we will need hard–shell boots, crampons, and ice axes for Spring Hill, The Heart and Misery Hill. It's a two–day climb, with the overnight on a level section at Helen Lake. The morning after, you climb from there to the summit and descend all the way to the truck at the Bunny Flat parking lot. The route–finding is straightforward. The climb seems doable, especially if we're both in shape and we catch good weather," I said, trying not to get too excited.

"That sounds possible. I'll check at the shop to be sure rentals are available and buy the book. And I'll start getting myself in shape. If I run into a glitch, I'll let you know. But for now, I'm in," he said.

A month later, I flew to California with my fly-fishing gear and my hard-shell boots, crampons, and ice axe, and Ben and I enjoyed a great week fly-fishing the Upper Sacramento and McCloud Rivers near his home in Mt. Shasta. Each day was better than the one before until there was only enough time left for our climb. On that morning, we drove to the Forest Service office for our backcountry permit and to the mountaineering shop in town where Ben rented his equipment for the next two days.

That afternoon, we drove back to McBride Springs, our campground on the Mt. Shasta approach road, and prepared for our climb. With all the gear out, Ben tried on the boots and crampons, and tramped around camp to get the feel of them. Hard-shell climbing boots provided more support up his calf, but they were much heavier than street shoes, and climbing steep snow for hours, much of it with a heavy pack, could cause great pain. Whether it would was still an unknown.

"How do they feel, Ben? How's your foot?" I asked.

"Actually, pretty good. No telling if it will be the same after hours of climbing, but for now, okay," he replied. I was relieved.

On top of his concerns about how his foot would hold up, the climb itself must have been on his mind. We'd backpacked together in Alaska nearly 30 years before, but since then, his forays into backcountry had been day hikes into less visited fly-fishing spots. Without any prior experience at altitude, a 14,000-foot peak was a considerable first attempt. Looking up from our camp that afternoon, the snow-covered mountain seemed friendly and close against a bluebird sky under mid-July sun. But

I knew from experience that the scale, distances, and pitch were actually far greater than they appeared from so far away. From McBride Springs, stretches that looked as though they'd take you an hour to climb could take three hours or more, even with good weather. Snow pitches that appeared to be hillside slopes loomed as 60-degree angles when you stood on them. With poor weather, the level of difficulty rises and climbing times increase. That's what makes climbing a mountain like Mt. Shasta exciting. It is also what focuses attention.

As I packed my gear, my mind was so clogged with what I had to remember I couldn't find my toothbrush, which made me question my ability to remember more important things later on. I was the one with some big mountain experience, although all of it was with friends who had climbed the routes before. I'd been the one asking the questions, and now Ben was, and I was the one doing my best to provide confidence-building but honest answers. I worried about getting an early start. It was cold that night, so I slept in the tent and Ben in his truck. The night sky, clear and star-filled, gave me hope for bright sun in the morning.

But in the morning all had changed. The last 10 days had been cloudless, but now clouds hung in the west and north and were building. A storm was approaching. But these were the last few days of my visit, so we were committed to the attempt, or at least as far as we could get.

We drove farther up the mountain road, to the point where they stop plowing, at Bunny Flat, where climbers park and begin their ascent. Even in mid-summer, at 7,000 feet, the roadside snow banks rose above Ben's truck. We shouldered our packs and left the parking lot at 7:15 a.m., headed for Horse-Camp, the single-room stone hut near a spring where climbers get water. We crunched along fully laden over the snow, ice axes and crampons secured to our packs. The route wound up through patches of forest scattered over slopes of open snow. There was no wind yet, but the overcast had begun to descend and obscure the mountain. By the time we got to Horse Camp, a half–hour later, the cloud bank had thickened and settled. The stone cabin was hunched down in the snow, covered to its eaves. The front door was at the bottom of a descending, shoveled corridor with walls of snow six feet high on both sides. We walked down the burrow into a dark and damp room.

Inside, we met a party that had just been turned back by a whiteout at about 13,000 feet. They joked lightly with one another, as if in relief to be off the mountain safely. One of them, a blonde woman with a friendly smile, shared a book off the cabin shelf with Ben. "There's a lot of interesting history in here," she said, handing it to him.

"Ben," I said. "Why don't we take it outside, where there's more light and we can keep an eye on the weather?"

On a bench outside, Ben browsed the book while I worried about resting too long and wondered if rain was going to cancel our climb.

"The Modoc Indians believe Mt. Shasta to be the origin of humanity, that people were born from the spirits on the mountain," he said. Then he added, "I hope those spirits will be with us."

As he finished a section, raindrops splattered the pages. We went back inside to return the book to its shelf and asked the caretaker about weather reports.

"Right now, they're indefinite, only indicating unsettled weather, which could mean almost anything. You should be all right if you have good gear. Just keep in mind what can happen with weather at higher altitudes," he said.

Ben wanted to wait and see what the weather did. I was worried about having enough time to make it to our night camp at

Helen Lake and nervously walked to the top of the first rise to calm myself and get a better look at what was ahead. The view wasn't promising, and it wasn't long either. Fog blanketed everything. But the rain wasn't heavy, and the air was still. I hiked back down to the cabin and found Ben without a boot on, rubbing his bare foot.

"Ben, the rain's not heavy and there's no wind. How's your foot?" I said.

"It's getting used to the boot, so it's sore. Can't say if it will adjust or get worse," he replied. "Are you okay with waiting here for a bit? It'll let us see what the weather's doing, and also give me a chance to rest my foot."

"Sure. But not so long that we can't make it to Helen Lake with light left to make camp and have dinner," I replied. We should make the decision to go ahead or not within the hour. Are you okay with that?"

"Yeah," Ben said, continuing to rub his foot.

The mountain wasn't being friendly, but it wasn't raging in anger either. Killing time, I fidgeted with gear and checked the guidebook repeatedly; Ben massaged his foot. An hour later, there was still no clear sign which way the weather would go. But Ben's foot was better, and we decided to keep climbing. If we'd known what we were climbing into, we wouldn't have.

We began to wind our way up slowly through the final stands of fir at the tree line. Thankfully the rain stopped, but the fog descended and we quickly found ourselves suspended in a ghostly stillness, unable to see more than about 30 feet. Off to our right, a climber we'd seen at Horse Camp carrying a snowboard disappeared and reappeared in the shifting veil. The thick fog distorted distance and depth perception.

Leaving the trees behind in the fog, we groped our way to the base of Misery Hill, a series of steep switchbacks below Helen

Lake, and discovered why it was so named.

The gradient increased sharply, permitting only short, kicked–in steps. Breathing heavily, I found a rhythm and kept grinding slowly up the slope, figuring that if I stopped I might not want to start again. I was so focused on each step and the chuffing monotony of my breaths that I didn't notice when the visibility shrank to 20 feet, then 15. When I paused, I realized I wasn't aware of how long I'd been slogging or when I'd last seen Ben.

"Ben," I called out in the fog, thinking he had to be near by. I felt the mist floating up the slope. After a wait, still no reply. *Did his foot get too painful? Did he stop or turn back?* "Ben!" I shouted, then held my breath, listening for his call, counting the seconds. *Is he lost? How far back is he?* Still no answer.

"Ben!" I screamed, frantically trying to reach in all directions at once. Then I held my breath again, straining to hear what I hoped for. But the only sound was the creaking of my crampons. *Is he hurt? Will I be able to find him?*

After a nerve–wracking wait, finally a reply. "Hugh, I hear you," floated up from the depths of fog. Flooded with relief, I felt my tension release.

When I caught my breath, I shouted, "Should I come down to you?"

"No. I'll come up," he answered faintly.

I had just broken the first commandment of lead climbing—don't ever leave your partners behind. Standing on the slope waiting, I realized that this route, Avalanche Gulch, the easiest one up Mt. Shasta, when combined with unfriendly weather, presented challenges enough.

"How are you doing, Ben?" I asked when he caught up.

"All right, I guess," he replied. "I just couldn't keep up."

"From now on, we'll set the pace together," I said, adding, "How's your foot?"

"Okay, so far."

For a few moments, we just stood there, listening to our breathing. In full sun, we could have seen the top of Spring Hill and gotten a fair estimate of how long it would take to climb to it. But poor visibility made such approximations impossible. Also, as the slope increases, measures of altitude gain mean more than measures of overland distance. But surrounded by clouds, as we were, it was also impossible to gauge our rate of ascent. Visibility shrank to a 10-foot radius. I kept checking my watch anyway, as the numbers on its face were now my only connection to the world we had come from, where we could see, to the world we were climbing into, where we couldn't.

Ben looked grim to me. I must have to him also. Neither of us spoke, each absorbed in our own questions. *"Will this lift or will it get worse? If it does get worse, will we be able to get down safely?"*

Suddenly we heard voices, and right away two men stepped from the gauze.

"Hello there!" one said. "How are you doing?"

"Okay so far, but I wish we could see where we are," I replied.

"That goes for both of us. Are you headed for Helen Lake?" he asked.

"Yes," I replied.

"We spent the night there last night. This is my brother," he said, pointing to his partner. "He turned fifty-eight today."

"Happy birthday. Nice to meet both of you," I said. "How's your climb been so far?"

"We got above Helen Lake this morning and got turned back by the weather," he said. "We couldn't see in the fog and had no idea where we were or even our direction."

"Kind of like here," I said.

"Yes, exactly," he replied. But, having gone up, we now have a better feel for the distance and direction going down. Well, we wish you better weather. Good luck."

"Thanks. Have a safe descent," I said as cheerfully as I could. We watched them disappear quickly into the fog, their happy chattering landing clearly on my envious ears.

On we climbed, the gradient steeper now. Thirty steps in creaking crampons, planting the ice axe with each one. Then rest, repeat. I looked at Ben, sitting in the snow.

"How're you doing, Ben?"

"I wonder what we're doing up here," he replied flatly. It was a statement, not a question, a statement with a lot of grave thinking behind it. Now I knew why he'd been so quiet.

"Well, we can turn back any time we have to. We can walk back down to Horse Camp with the remaining light, and when we have to, we should. We just can't predict what the weather will do."

I was hoping that what I had said did two things: convinced him that I really was ready to turn around if we had to and wasn't so rabid that I'd march us off a cliff in the fog and that I didn't think we had to turn around yet, but that, like him, it was an option I was keeping handy.

"Let's keep talking," he said, standing up.

"For sure," I replied, as we both resumed climbing.

Farther up, we met a man who had been turned back above Red Banks, a prominent cliff band far above Helen Lake, only an hour and a half from the summit.

"I started from Bunny Flat at two a.m.," he said. "And climbed all night, intending to summit and return in one long day. I live in Mt. Shasta, and I've climbed the mountain eight times and made it to the top six times."

"How far are we from Helen Lake?" I asked him.

"If you go directly, without wandering in this fog too much, it's only about two hours," he said. "If the weather holds, and especially if it improves, you should be able to make it there with plenty of time to set up camp."

He obviously knew the mountain, so his encouragement to continue meant something. And we did, with me somewhat buoyed by the knowledge that about two hours up was our destination, Helen Lake. I hoped the same was true for Ben.

But shortly after we said goodbye it started to snow. Lightly at first, but then it picked up and blew downslope into our faces before sweeping up and off the mountain. We pulled on another layer and hats and gloves, and for the first time I started to think it might be time to turn around. The snow was dry, and the wind came in gusts laden with intimidation. There were lulls when the snow let up, but the slope was getting steeper and we still couldn't see up or down.

Everywhere was white: foreground, background, the air itself. Ben and I kept together, heads down, the crunch of our boots confirming each other's presence. If it weren't for the fact that the slope was continually up, our feet wouldn't have known where to land. In the flat light and limited visibility I couldn't tell by looking at the ground which way it angled. We were climbing by feel. Or at least our feet were.

We kept climbing, side by side, resting every 30 steps. I kept checking my watch, using the last climber's estimate of two hours to approximate the distance to Helen Lake. Then the gradient sharpened even more. Along with it came stronger wind, gusts hard enough to stop me and turn my face away. The tipping point to abandon our climb was close. But the wind and snow got no worse and we kept climbing. Our labor kept us warm, and we still had time to get down if we had to. We just couldn't see where we were, and I hoped we hadn't drifted too far off route. I kept checking my watch. An hour passed. The snow swirled around us, visibility nil. As we repeated our 30 steps and rest cycle, again and again, we closed in on two hours. The lake had to appear soon.

Finally the pitch lessened, then leveled off, and we knew we'd made it to the flat that holds Helen Lake. The lake is usually frozen year round, and after tramping around to get our bearings, we decided that the location of the actual lake itself was the lowest spot on the flat, buried under 20 or 30 feet of snow.

That's when the storm hit full force.

The snow was horizontal, the wind steady at about 20 miles an hour, the visibility less than 10 feet. We found a waist-high wall of snow blocks built by a previous climber, and though ready to rest and eat, we couldn't because of the weather. Ben threw on his last layer, a huge down parka a friend of his had worn while guiding clients in the Himalayas. I ate some trail mix for a quick spurt of energy. In the 30 seconds it took to do so, my hands went numb. We swapped photos of each other standing by the snow-block wall in the gale.

"I don't want to spend the night here in this, Ben. What do you say to heading down?"

"No problem with me, bro. Let's go."

We removed our crampons, and within 10 minutes of our arrival we were glissading back down the steep grade, sliding on our rear ends and using our ice axes to slow our speed.

On the way, it stopped snowing. When we stood up at the bottom, it was to breaking clouds, racing by overhead as if in time-lapse photography, while around us the air was calm. Gradually, bits of blue appeared and disappeared, and we both stood in silence watching the storm move off, marveling at the change occurring before our eyes as more and more of the valley came into view.

Nodding at the crest we'd just left, which we could now see

clearly, Ben asked, "You really want to go back there, don't you?"

Pretty sure he'd had enough, I said, "Yes, I'm not ready to leave. The view to the summit is possible now. If I left my pack here, I could climb it and be back in just over an hour. Would you mind waiting for me?"

"No," he said. "It's a relief just to sit here." So I dropped my pack and for the second time, climbed to Helen Lake.

The view was improving by the minute. Stepping in my own tracks, and with glorious visibility, Spring Hill was much easier this time and I ascended quickly. The wind was still, and far below me I could see Ben resting by his pack. Within what seemed like a few short minutes, I once again stepped onto the flat that held Helen Lake. Nearby, I spoke with a couple from Calgary who had weathered it out there for two days, waiting for a summit chance. Ben and I hadn't even seen their tent. While we spoke, the storm moved off completely and opened views that had me gazing in rapture.

The three towns around the base of Shasta stood out clearly, and in the distance the snow–capped range of the Trinity Alps lined the horizon. The steep snow face of The Heart rose to Red Banks. I was tempted to linger. But it was now 4:00, time to leave if we were to climb back down to Bunny Flat before nightfall.

Glissading back down, I couldn't stop thinking about how I could convince Ben that we should stay, that we really had a good chance to summit now. But I also prepared myself for the return to the truck, sure that Ben would want that. We had given it a good try, as good as could be expected from a couple of guys new to this mountain, and I was willing to give the mountain its due. Climbing any 14,000 foot mountain is no small feat and this one had given us a fair share of its wrath.

When I reached Ben, he looked me right in the eye and, before I could speak, said, "Let's go up." The smiles we exchanged showed teeth that hadn't seen daylight in years. And so, for the third time, I climbed to Helen Lake, this time with a shard of hope that we just might reach the summit after all.

We set up our tent by the same snow–block wall we had deserted so recently and walked over to say hello to the Canadians. After their long wait, they were also anxious to climb and were as glad as we were that tomorrow would be the day.

Returning to our camp, we made our dehydrated dinner, maritime surprise, melting snow from fresh snow slides for water. As we finished, the shadows crept onto the frozen, buried lake, and we prepared for a cold night. In the 180–degree view, we watched the lights come on in the towns of Weed, Mt. Shasta, and McCloud and felt the earth turn toward night.

When I crawled into my sleeping bag, I kept on most of the clothes I'd brought. The remaining ones joined me in the bag to keep them warm, my boots especially. Ben was wearing the green down parka his friend had lent him. I tossed for a while but before I finally fell asleep I could hear Ben tossing and shifting.

In the morning, the water bottles we'd placed outside the tent were frozen solid. It was just before 6:00, much later than I wished. Looking up the south face, I saw the Canadians already approaching Red Banks, the cliff band high up. I wanted to get going right away. We'd now be caught in full sun on the snow face with the sun's glare both frying us and softening the snow, slowing our ascent. If the snow got too soft and we fell through to our knees, our climb was over. The sooner we left, the farther we'd get before that would happen. Time to hustle.

We quickly cooked a pot of oatmeal and made tea, leaving the dishes for later. While packing lunches, water, and a shell layer in daypacks, I discovered that I'd shattered a lens in my sunglasses, rolling over them during the night. I covered the empty frame with duct tape to protect that eye from snow blindness. I'd have to climb one-eyed. With crampons on and ice axes in hand, Ben and I approached the foot of the main snow face.

The goal was to summit shortly after noon and descend to camp, then pack up the tent and sleeping bags and make it back to Bunny Flat by late afternoon. With our late start we'd be later, but still within the margin of safety. If all went well.

The main snow face, called The Heart, steepened quickly, reaching maximum pitch within a few minutes. Standing up, I could reach out and touch the slope without leaning. In the shade of early morning, the crampons clung to the frozen snow. We could step lightly in a slow rhythm, climbing diagonally up and across the slope to a certain point, then turn and zigzag up in the other direction with our ice axes always on the uphill side to use as a brake in case we fell.

Ben and I huffed with the exertion in altitude, but we made steady progress, side by side, up the massive snow face, quietly finding our own pace. Although it was strange at first, I got used to climbing with one eye. The higher we got, the wider the view opened, and I was often tempted to pause longer than I should to soak in the vistas. With no wind, the crunch of the crampons kept time with our breathing. I looked over occasionally to see how Ben was doing, and he looked fine, as though he'd actually found a mantra in the repetitive motion. Looking upslope, I could see the dawn's shadow line still much higher up. As we climbed to meet it, I tried to prepare myself for the sun's brilliant reflection off this wall of snow.

We measured our progress with our distance to Red Banks, high above us. Small pieces of ice were falling from it, and bouncing past at high speed with an eerie musical, tinkling sound, breaking the otherworldly heavy silence. A sound only mountaineers know. I kept looking at my watch to gauge our climbing rate. It was important to know how quickly we were using up our time. The view expanded the higher we climbed, now stretching to the southern horizon. As the steep angle fell away below us our exposure increased. Better not to look down. Thirty steps, stop, rest. Repeat.

The sun's dazzling rays caught us about two thirds of the way up the southern face, and we watched dawn's shadow racing down the face below us. Within a few minutes, Ben and I both shed a layer. To do so, I removed my sunglasses, and the brilliant reflection off the snow stabbed my eyes. I put the sunglasses back on quickly, thankful for the duct tape. Without it, snow blindness was a given.

Three rests above, we shed clothes a second time, down now to the base layer, which would prevent sun poisoning. All skin that could be covered had to be. But we couldn't turn away from the steep angle we were climbing, and our faces, smeared with sunscreen, still burned. The snow softened with the sun, slowing our progress, and I quickened my pace. I didn't want to be caught climbing on a slope this steep in deep, soft snow. We had to reach Red Banks before that happened. But the quicker I went the more I sweated and the more water I drank. I wished we'd started earlier.

"How are you doing, Ben?" I asked.

"Much better than I thought I would," he replied. "I found a rhythm. The softer snow is slower, though, and I want to get to Red Banks."

"Me too," I said. "Are your face and eyes okay?"

"So far. There'll be flatter ground above Red Banks, which should ease the sun's reflection."

"Gotcha. Let's get there."

"Righty–o, bro."

At least now we knew what to expect. The climbing slowed

the higher we got, but at a rate that I thought would allow us to get to Red Banks, which now seemed within reach. That thought inspired me, and I climbed higher each stretch before resting, reeling myself up to the cliff band. An hour passed. Then another, and we were close. My lungs were clear, wringing oxygen from each breath.

Finally, Red Banks was in front of us, a massive cliff band of red sandstone. Ben and I paused, gaping upward.

"How you doing, Ben? How's your foot?" I asked.

"Amazingly, there's no pain. Or at least I can't feel it."

"I'm really glad for that. The route goes off to the right, around the cliff, winding up through that slot," I said pointing.

"And the snow's not too soft yet," Ben said, taking a slug of water.

"Which is just fine with me," I said, returning my water bottle to its holster.

"Great. Let's get going. I can't wait to see the view, bro."

From there the slope rose, but with a much lower angle than before. So even though the snow was softer, we covered ground quickly. We stomped up around the cliff band through the slot formed with The Thumb, a prominent tower to the east. The cut provided welcome shade, and I felt my face cooling. The route from there rose slightly, crossing a saddle before the final pitch to the summit. It was noon, with still a ways to go. I checked my rising hope, afraid to jinx our fortune, but inside I was churning.

As we trudged across the saddle, a cloud of undercast clung to the north flank of the mountain beneath us, like a floating blanket of cotton. The cone of Shastina, Mt. Shasta's sister peak, appeared to our west. A plume of gases rose from the fumarole, the still active core of Mt. Shasta's younger sibling, and the acrid smell of sulfur hung in the air, whispering "volcano". We kept moving, turning east, spurred by the sight of the last rise to the summit before us. A plainly visible and steep ramp rose diagonally from its base to the summit plateau.

Twenty minutes of trudging brought us to Misery Hill, which, at 13,000 feet, blocks a view of the true summit beyond. In the higher altitude and thinner air, with 6,000 feet already scaled, climbing Misery Hill became just that. We lost steam the higher we went, but with the prize within reach, we clomped our way up in the soft snow and bright sun. About two hours later, we stepped onto the exposed rocks of the summit plateau and crossed a few hundred yards to the summit.

In the photo, Ben and I are sitting on a rock, our arms around each other's shoulders, burned faces gleaming, eyes squinting in the sun. You can hear our laughing smiles as Ben raises his thumb in the triumphant joy of brotherhood. On the back, he wrote: "Couldn't have done it without you. I'll always remember this. Love, Bro."

They call it "the sport of suffering", plenty of which we both had endured. Glissading down The Heart erased it all with the exhilaration of its lightning ride. Eight hours from Helen Lake to get to the summit, less than two to return. We made it to the truck by early evening, and by twilight were casting flies to rising trout on the Upper Sacramento River, which only a few hours before had been 11,000 feet below us.

And I ask: How can a person seek more from earthly experience?

Absence Letter

May 2000

Dear Monique,

Tonight at dinner Kelsey asked what today was. When I told him "Wednesday, May 11," he said, "When is Mommy coming home?"

"On Wednesday," I replied, omitting "the eighteenth".

He said, with that knowing twinkle and a smile, "Oh, you mean she's coming home today?" We all laughed.

Graham glazed his clay pot today in art, and Kelsey made a colorful butterfly for his project, which he immediately gave to Graham.

"I didn't have such a good time with Ryan today, because Ryan wouldn't share his toys," Kelsey said.

Graham said, "Seth was in a bad mood and kept accusing me of doing stuff."

We played ball after dinner and had a great time. Graham read his storybox book to me before bed. He reads with much less tension already. I called Janet and Terri to thank them for their help.

A man would have to be crazy to think that his wife was going to raft a western river through desert for a week, with a women–only crew, and not come back a changed person. Floating through canyons that date from the Paleozoic, gazing up toward heavens at stars that leap out at you, all the while suspended on a ribbon of water that's been doing the carving and has itself been looking at those same stars for hundreds of millions of years can have a powerful effect on how someone subsequently looks at herself and her life.

Considering myself of sound mind, I am prepared for encountering a different you at the terminal than the one who left Monday. As such, I imagine you to be reentering a play that has continued in your absence and needing a bit of orientation to synchronize your "trip being" with your persona before you left.

Whatever angle you come in on, I'll be there. We may not "see" each other for a while, but we'll be there just the same.

All around us now we are surrounded by that most beautiful of green, the tender young green of promise. It made me reach for the seed catalogue.

I can't wait to see you.

Common Ground

July 2000

It's amazing, even after many years, how time spent fishing with someone has an eternal quality. Perhaps that is why so many anglers pair up for so long and why, after a falling out, they refer to it in terms that could describe a divorce, and perhaps why, also, there is such a sense of loss when one partner moves away, leaving the other adrift, no longer with that so rewarding companionship. It's about the nature of partnerships, fishing partnerships, and fly–fishing partnerships in particular, with their sense of ritual and tradition. It especially applies to those partnerships that have grown over time, or even, more poignantly, to those held since childhood.

Because we didn't have parents who were present much, my fishing life with my brothers has become the common ground through which we've remained in touch. Sometimes the contact isn't frequent, but there's been enough contact in storage to leap the gaps that occur.

My brother Tim wanted to show me his boat. I knew that was one of the reasons for his invitation to spend the day with him on it. He also wanted to show me his skills as a captain, to have me see him in action performing an ability he had worked hard to acquire. After leaving college, he went to California and crewed on charter boats, eventually earning his captain's license. He knew I knew he was a savvy fisherman. The enlarged photos of trophy fish on his walls and the years of stories from places all over the Western hemisphere proved that. But being a good fisherman and being someone people want to fish with are two different things. I knew he was the former and hoped he had become the latter.

He was changing. In the past, he had taunted authority, coming close to jail time. As much as I wanted to enjoy my time with him I held a nagging worry about what would go wrong. Outings together in the past had involved speeding cars, risky behavior in boats, and conflicts with the community. My first priority on this trip was making sure there were no such adverse encounters. My wife had the same concern, and she made me promise to call from the boatyard each day.

Tim drove as we headed toward Long Island Sound on the eastern Connecticut shore, where his boat was moored. The windows were rolled down, the setting July sun cast bright rays in the rearview mirrors, and both of us wore sunglasses. It was the moment when you realize that summer is no longer coming. It is here.

We passed a thermos of coffee between us, slugging nearly all of it, and our lively talk was full of expectation. Tim even had a plan. Because we were going to arrive at the boat with plenty of light left, he wanted to take it out into The Race, where the tidal rip passes the head of Fishers Island, and try a few casts. With plenty of solstice sun, we'd be able to get out and back before dark. The next morning we'd have a better idea of where to spend our day together fishing. It would also give me my first chance to practice with the weighted lines on the saltwater fly rods. I listened to all this carefully. For Tim to have a plan was something new. I could feel my grip on the coffee mug relax.

As he drove, he told me about his work. He'd spent the last five years getting himself set up in business, and his painting company was running well enough to permit him these getaways. He'd built a positive reputation, and plenty of customers lined up for his work. His crew was dependable and responsible enough to complete quality work even when he wasn't around. When I remarked that he was lucky to have such a crew, he made a point of telling me that it was more his hard work training and managing the crew than it was luck. I knew from his answer that he wanted me to understand that he had worked hard and played by the rules to get this far.

The boat was docked in a small boatyard in Noank, sandwiched between a harborside restaurant and a much larger marina. There was a parking lot on shore for the owners of the dozen boats at the dock and a cabana that housed the showers and the pay phone. We loaded our coolers and tackle, and while the engines were warming up, Tim showed me his prize possession.

I'm not a saltwater man, but even with my limited knowledge of fishing vessels, I was impressed. Over its 36 feet, the craft reflected the purpose for which it was built: the pursuit of large fish in comfort and efficiency. The captain's dashboard housed the Loran for finding the boat's position and heading, sonar to read the bottom and locate fish, and a ship–to–shore radio, complete with marine band weather reporting. Below these electronics, the gauges on the dashboard showed the status of the twin 350 horsepower engines beneath the main deck. There were two live bait wells, one on each side of the main deck along the hull, where seawater pumped through them. A tuna door, a section of the transom, which swung out, allowed large fish to be hauled aboard at water level, without having to hoist them over the side.

The tower rose overhead, complete with helm, engine controls, and a canopy of its own. The cabin below the deck was outfitted with a shower, head, stove, refrigerator, and two beds built into the V of the bow, paneled in mahogany. It was, as Tim said, his "fishing machine."

Under warm sun and clear skies, with no wind and flat water, we wove our way out of the harbor through moored boats. The few outboards that buzzed nearby were speeding to spots beyond us, local guys out after work, trying to squeeze in a little fishing.

We cruised toward The Race and, once on the open water, Tim asked me to take the helm while he rigged the fly rods. He showed me the knot he tied to attach the doubled–over shock tippet to the flies. This knot absorbs the force of a strike and keeps the line from breaking. We spotted a few small schools of active striped bass, but by the time we got to them the baitfish they were chasing had sounded, the stripers with them, leaving us throwing long lines to vast expanses of quiet water.

Fly–fishing like this was new to me, and Tim gave me instructions, careful not to seem too much the boss or the expert. The change in color between the heavy, leaded, forward section of line and the regular running line was the marker. Strip the line in until that color change is just below the rod tip, carefully piling the stripped line in coils at your feet. Then lift the line off the water with one back cast, and send the leaded line forward. If done right, the momentum in the leaded line lifts the coils on the deck, sending them to their full length. More than one false cast causes the heavy forward section to pile up midair, ruining the cast. When I launched the cast, I had to avoid stepping on the coils of rapidly exiting line under my feet. Stopped in such a fashion, the hook out in front of you suddenly reverses direction, coming back on a collision course with your face. The saying goes that experience can be a hard teacher; she tests first and teaches afterward, but Tim's pointers were keeping me from learning solely from that rough hand. He was taking the time to offer his experience, not in his old way, with exaggerated stories of his exploits, but in a way that was helpful to me. I was surprised at this change, and, registering my surprise, felt myself break into a smile.

Even from far off, there was no mistaking the location of The Race. The standing waves far offshore indicated the point where the tidal rip flowed around the head of Fishers Island. The ocean floor suddenly came near the surface, and the combination of these two forces produced the namesake current. The power of this sweep was clear and present. The bottom, strewn with huge rock slabs, was plainly visible. Kelp attached to the rocks was whipping wildly. Both engines were running just to keep us in place. A foaming wave broke from the bow as we split the river of salt water racing to the sea. A large green buoy, partially submerged, was leaning steeply in the current rushing around it.

On the outgoing tide, The Race could be great fishing. Baitfish schooled in the quiet water just ahead of the current's pull, and the bluefish, striped bass, and bonita followed them. Trying to cast across the current and let the fly swing in front of these predators, while keeping my balance on the rolling deck, required full focus.

What kept me working so hard was the sight of Tim hustling to handle the boat. Using the green buoy as a reference point, he spun the wheel to ferry us back and forth across the current. At the same time, he was busy at the controls, changing gearbox and throttle to adjust our position; the port engine now in neutral, now ahead, the starboard one now reversed, now neutral. Because the depth finder was ineffective in such shallow water, he kept looking over the side to check for himself. He was alert, gauging distance to the buoy and the strength and direction of the current, trying to keep or change our location as he played out his hunches. He handled the boat adeptly, fully absorbed in response to the water, his knowledge, and his intuition. He was enjoying himself.

We kept at it until dusk nudged us reluctantly homeward, but despite our best efforts in tandem, I didn't catch anything. By the time we returned to the boatyard, night was falling. Tim skillfully negotiated the narrow channel, backed the boat into our slip, and we tied it up. In the darkness, we listened to the weather forecast on the radio and the water lapping at the hull. We went to bed feeling tired but hopeful.

Lying in the dark, he spoke first of the boat: how he'd been able to afford it, what he'd done to improve it, and the success he'd had with it so far. That changed into talk of his daughter and his relationship with her and his ex–wife. Finally, he brought himself to the present with talk of his current wife and their plans for the future. He was changing, and his way of looking at his life and the people in it was changing also. It was as if he was catching me up on his life over the last 20 years and coming to peace with it himself. By the time he was done, he'd been talking over an hour. I hadn't even asked him a question.

In the morning, the thick fog limited visibility, and we had to rely on instruments to make our way out of the harbor. With the diesels slapping rhythmically, we crept through the mist, eyes riveted to the radar screen. While I tried to read the screen, Tim would point out features, tell me what they probably were, and estimate our distance to them. At one point he said, "There's going to be a buoy ten feet off the port side in a few seconds." I was impressed when it slid into view after a brief pause.

As we moved into the bay the morning breeze began to break up the fog, and by the time we got to The Race the sun had finished the job. Once again, we tried the tactics of the day before, hovering over the lip of the current where it broke from Long Island Sound on its mad rush to the Atlantic. Side to side and front to back, dropping back with the rushing water, we surfed our way down through it and motored back to the top to try again. Again and again we tried until my fingers were numb from casting and Tim's face was strained with the effort of boat handling. We'd been trying for enough time to consider quitting when a few other boats arrived. Tim recognized a captain and pulled alongside to swap notes. It was the same story all over; no one was catching any fish.

We drifted off, and after a moment's deliberation, Tim steered a new course to what we both hoped would be more productive water. What followed was proof of his best intentions—an intensive tour of every spot he knew within a five-mile radius. We worked along the island's shore, tried shallow coves, and cast repeatedly behind jetties as the morning petered toward noon and our hopes waned. Every once in a while Tim would fish, but mostly he would captain, maneuvering the boat to give us every advantage he could coax from the blank water. With each new location proving as futile as the last, his countenance had new lines in it.

Noon became afternoon, hot under a blazing sun. We stripped to shorts and lathered on the sunblock. Even with dark sunglasses, the glare off the water had me squinting. After what seemed like an eternal stint of casting over water I no longer had any hope for, we cut the engines and just stood there, staring at each other, sweat running off our faces. Suddenly, Tim's face broke into a sly grin and he said, "Time to try the lighthouse." Just as quickly, he turned the ignition and off we headed.

The lighthouse was an imposing sight, perched on a mound of granite blocks well offshore. It now operated remotely, although it had once been occupied, and the fact that it was deserted, combined with its stark appearance and isolation, gave it an eerie feeling.

A breeze came up, raising our hopes along with it, and as we pulled near the rocks Tim said that the stripers would try to pin the baitfish against the rocks, so we'd need to get the fly in close for it to be any good. The now changing tide was moving toward the light in strong surges. As we drifted toward the rocks, I cast as close as I could ahead of the boat, trying to manage the cast, keep the line away from the props, and maintain my balance. On the second pass, the line didn't come up from below the hull and after a tug I knew it was wrapped in the propeller shaft. Tim cut the engines. Fortunately, our line of drift had changed enough so that it was going to carry us by and not into the rocks. As we floated by the lighthouse, almost close enough to leap onto it, Tim started taking off his hat, shirt, and shoes.

"What are you doing?" I asked.

"I'm going over. I bet I can untangle that line. Keep an eye out for other boats and signal them while I'm down there."

With that, he opened the tuna door and dove off the stern.

It was strange to be standing all alone on my brother's boat, rocking in the swell, with him underneath it like a native diver. Having just worked intensely together for the last six hours, I felt stranded in the sudden quiet. My thoughts, smeared in the heat, skipped like a bad tape. I wondered what I could do to fix my mistake, and marveled at his line of action. He popped up, took a few deep breaths, and dove again. After about six tries, he said, "I think I'll have it this time." Sure enough, the line came free. Tim came back on board, started the engines, and we steered again into position near the rocks.

The swells were higher now, but stripers had arrived and were slashing the surface, pinning the baitfish in a frenzy. Deftly,

Tim put us in position, and I launched a cast that only the day's practice could have prepared me for. The first twitch of my retrieve was answered with a violent yank that traumatized my rod and the arm attached to it. Pure luck kept me hooked up through the initial explosion until the fish's fight began to assume a more predictable nature. I thought to look for Tim. He was looking back, smiling in a curve to match my rod's.

In the photograph I have from the day, I'm smiling, holding up the striped bass, with the lighthouse in the background. And even though Tim took the picture, he's in it too, in my mind's eye, reflected in our common ground.

At the Bus Stop

September 2003

Every now and then life gives you one of those clearly defined moments of change that make you stop and reflect, and this fall has brought one that's particularly poignant. Our youngest son has stopped taking the bus to school, and I'm no longer waiting for it with him.

Because the school where I teach opens later than the school where he went until this year, I could keep him company until his bus came, and we'd while away the time having a lot of fun.

His older brother, Graham, was part of this morning routine until two falls ago, when he started high school one town away. With just Kelsey, I still could enjoy the routine, so there didn't seem to be that much of a change. It always began with the boys riding on the tailgate of our hatchback down our dirt road. They loved this activity and would insist, even in winter, on dangling their legs off the back and dragging their feet in the snow as we bounced toward the bus stop.

Once there, it became a matter of choosing a game to play. Occasionally, when it was just too cold or rainy outside, we'd stay in the car and listen to reports on NPR. But this rarely happened, because our games always involved movement that kept us warm.

As a trio, we'd usually throw a tennis ball in some form of "keep away." Sometimes it was a long–tailed ball called a foxtail. We'd challenge ourselves to throw lefty and laugh at our awkward efforts. When there was snow on the ground we'd heave snowballs at one another or pick targets in the river swirling below the road, threading our missiles through bare tree branches.

Sometimes a neighbor would stop and chat. We'd always yell "CAR!" when one was coming and get ourselves off the road. We knew about what time to expect the yellow bus, and when we saw it we'd yell "BUS!" and race to the open tailgate of the car; the boys would shoulder their backpacks and grab their lunches. I'd always give them a kiss and tell them to have a good day. The bus would stop, and Mr. Ed, the driver, and I would exchange waves and the boys would be gone.

Sometimes we'd be too late and we'd miss the bus, so then I'd drive them to their school. I remember feeling lucky having this morning time together with them sending them off on their day.

When Graham started high school, it became just Kelsey and me, but our routine changed only by including some new things to throw. We started to include golf balls, Frisbees, footballs, and just about every other "ball" you can think of. This was Kelsey's love of all ball sports showing itself. We also branched out to other activities.

One of these was walking the slack cable between the guardrail posts along the road. Kelsey started this one winter morning by getting up on a cable and balancing on a post, then walking the cable to the next post. When he reached the midpoint between posts the cable sagged, and his legs quivered while his arms windmilled overhead to help him keep his balance. In this flurry, he'd dash to the next post, where he would perch on its slanted top. Small clouds of condensation puffed from his mouth. He made it to the next post and to the one past that before falling. It was my turn.

Just getting two feet onto the cable was tough. Either I'd wobble uncontrollably and launch myself off or I'd just slip off the cable. What I found incredibly difficult Kelsey was performing as a warm-up. It was obvious that our measures of success were going to be different. On his turns, he'd almost always succeed in adding another post to his walk. Over 20 posts stretched out into what seemed impossible. I was still trying to make it to my first post. After a while, we'd return to our game of catch in the street, trying all sorts of variations. But each day he'd always lead us back to the cable walk. We kept at this for a couple of weeks.

Then one morning I watched as he hopped onto the cable and began a new attempt to break his record of five or six posts. From the start he was carrying his balance smoothly. He hardly wobbled as he surpassed his old record, and new, more distant posts kept appearing under his sneakers. Silently, with no distractions, he'd step from a post quickly onto the cable, take three quick steps, and come to roost on the next post. After a slight pause, during which he'd shift his feet so he could start on the same foot, he'd step out onto the cable again, barely waving his arms. In a perfectly symmetrical parabola, he'd dip down onto the cable like a wave and ride to the top of the next post.

Gliding down the cable, his wave joined the universal oscillation—the thrumming of life, from the 60 cycle hum of your refrigerator to the rhythm of the cicada's rasp to the ringing of silence in my ears—and became all there was. The swishing, rushing river below, with floating ice grating on the banks and current sweeping to the sea, went silent.

There was just Kelsey, dancing on the cable.

Neither of us said a word, as I watched him walk its full

length of 20 posts and then pirouette and return.

Of course I showered him with praise and, in his style, he smiled, pleased with himself, but said little, as if talking about it would somehow take it away. We stood for a few moments, just enjoying what he'd done. And then the bus appeared around the bend and it was time to part. I gave him a kiss, he got on, and we waved to each other from behind glass. We both smiled.

This fall, Kelsey joined Graham at the high school, and the days of waiting for the bus are gone. We've turned a corner in our lives, and the hurried pace of high school has taken over. And although freshman year has excitements all its own, the now more important business of getting ready for college has crowded the minutes that we have together.

But that morning, dancing on the cable, Kelsey gave us both a few that will be frozen in beauty forever.

The House

August 2005

My two brothers and a sister and I all shared a room, but when my sister turned thirteen, Mom decided it would be better if she had a room of her own. So she had a builder make a wall that divided up our common space into two spaces—one for our sister and one for me and my brothers.

But even though the room shift was a big change in our arrangements, it wasn't as important as the house itself, which seemed to hover over the changes as though they were minor cosmetic switches, which is what they were.

The house, which we called Kettle Creek after the street it faced, loomed like a fortress in our lives, sometimes a palace, sometimes a prison, always an institution. From its dank basement, with obsolete coal bins and asbestos–wrapped pipes, to the top of the chimney, where I'd climb occasionally and view Long Island Sound miles away, it was a collection of memories, objects, and even feelings that became the repository of our childhood. We played and fought in it, ran away from it, brought our trophies back to it, and experienced and remembered some of our tragedies there.

Even now, 35 years after leaving it, it still stands in our minds as the house, the quintessential abode, the dwelling of our consciousness, the point of departure from which we viewed the rest of the world. It remains the standard by which all other houses we've lived in are measured and, in a sense, our lives as well. In a tangible way, we measure how well we are doing by how closely the house we live in now resembles Kettle Creek in feel, atmosphere, and potential for wonder.

So when my wife and I found a house for sale that had the same crystal doorknobs on the same paneled doors, the same radiators fueled by the same hulking oil furnace, the same towering trees growing from the same expansive lawn, we knew we'd found our home. It dated from the same decade as Kettle Creek, the Thirties, had the same hardwood floors and plaster walls and even the same afternoon sunlight dappling the living room floor.

In the seven years we've lived in it, our house has become even richer than the memories we brought to it, made richer by the memories we've made in it together. The lawn, just like Kettle Creek's, has been the center for volleyball, badminton, golf, baseball, soccer, and even a tennis game our sons invented called "dirt Wimbledon." It has seen Slip 'N Slide, treasure hunts, and sparklers. Leaf piles and snow forts, branch forts, log forts and hole–in–the–ground forts have all come and gone.

The house has witnessed science projects of reeking jars of water, nascent rock bands practicing, skateboarding tricks in the basement, hours of homework, board games in the living room, and the raucous cavorting of family members of all ages during the holidays.

And now, when I come home to the empty house, its silence echoes with these people, their spirits, their lives. It's a happy silence for all it evokes, but it's simultaneously a profoundly melancholic emptiness, as of a grand life departed.

The Rope Swing

May 2006

The first time I saw it was a raw discovery, the kind that has "unique" written all over it. My wife and I and our two sons had been riding our bikes down past the old tunnel, following the old railroad bed just to see where it went. We emerged from a patch of woods to where the bed stopped at the river and the twisted, half–submerged girders of an old bridge. We stopped too, and looked around. A stream came into the river on the far side, forming a small peninsula of land out into the river. At the point of the V an immense sycamore tree with knotted, gnarly branches towered out over the water. From a limb perhaps 40 feet up hung a thick, long rope, straight down, nearly to the water's glimmering surface. It had two knots in it, one at the bottom and one about six feet up. Short boards nailed to the tree as ladder steps led up to a branch lower than the one the rope was tied to, but still a considerable way up.

Right away we were anxious to get to it, but first we had to cross the river. We laid down our bikes, kicked off our shoes, and waded in. The soft, golden bottom sand poured through our toes as we edged our way across and emerged onto the point at the base of the huge tree. I forget who went first, but we soon realized that the higher knot required a scary lunge from the branch you stood on to reach it. But it carried you out higher over the water than the first knot did, and you could hang from it stretched out and not hit the water on the swing, which was much easier on your arms. The bottom knot was easier to reach and gave you greater centrifugal force and therefore a higher arc, but you had to hold yourself up to it as you were swinging down or you'd hit the river at pretty much top speed. The momentum would cartwheel you across the water in a dizzying twirl. But if you were able to keep yourself scrunched up under the big bottom knot and not hit the water, the higher arc would launch you above the point where the rope was tied to the branch and you'd be well aware of yourself going up, not down, into the upper reaches of the tree's foliage. The descent was a mixture of nerves, joy, and finally triumph, with letting curiosity about the experience trump fear about its possible outcome. It was usually punctuated by a primal scream.

We spent the next hour practicing various combinations of launch height and mid–air maneuvers, and although the swing got more comfortable, it never got routine. We've returned a number of times, always finding no one else there, and that's helped me realize why the rope swing is so full of meaning.

Its beauty represents an American past you don't see much any more. There are no lines of cars, no people. It's a very private spot far from a road, which says two things: you have to really want to get there because it's hard to find and you have to be careful because help is a long way off. It's a setting for a memoir or a childhood story. It's where you go first with your parents and later, when you're older, with a brother and finally with a boy or girlfriend. It's a place you want to only share with special people.

It also represents an adventurous challenge. Just climbing the tree is tough, and if you fall from it you're going to get hurt. To leap holding the top knot is scary enough, but to launch yourself out over that water from so high up, holding the bottom knot, is to hold your heart in your throat and pray for help from the gods. You know it's going to be all right until, at the bottom of the swing, the centrifugal force is trying to strip you from the rope and skip you across the water, and then you're not so sure. With clenched fists and trembling muscles you arc swiftly to the apex, where you and the rope part company. You can count to three slowly before you hit the water, but you can't hear yourself over the sound of your screams. Safe in the river, you feel relieved and proud and still a bit frightened and you can't wait to do it again.

The connections the rope swing gives me with people are stronger than those from many other places. The bond of sharing the joy and the fear, of encouraging each other, of laughter together, of the freedom of water, space, and time converging so intensely, lasts forever. The pictures are frozen into my mind: airborne sons screaming with delight, the whomp and the telltale cherry-red skin from a faulty landing, the splash of the silver water and the swirl of the ocher current sweeping the sand. Just the words, "the rope swing" produce a strong image. A visual one for sure, but an emotional one too. One of days spent connected with and grounded in each other within the natural world. You know that generations now grown and moved away have probably done the same right here. That history soaks your experience to the point where, while there, you are absolutely conscious that you are shaping your own.

From places this special we all try to take items that remind us of the strong, powerful effect the location had on us. Hence the bustling trade in souvenirs. Somehow, we hope that the pair of moccasins will evoke the wonder of the two weeks we spent on the Maine coast or that the plastic bow and arrow will do the same for our trip to the Rockies. We hope the thing will stand for the experience, but we hope in vain.

No token can bring the rush of adrenaline as the swing plunges toward the water. And no trinket can even begin to encompass the stories of the people who've come here. The consciousness of life that happens here can't be brought home, but it can live in memory.

In the end, it's not anything material you take from such a place that gives it such impact, but what you leave there. And what you leave there is a piece of yourself, a piece of beauty within you that found its match in this special place. Your being senses this and wants to return in order to feel whole again. And you do, realizing that once you've been to such a special place you never completely come back.

Once More to the Falls

July 2009

In going back to a place where you spent some formative time there's always a risk that you'll find more than memories. And so it was when I returned with my teenage sons and wife to a swimming hole where I had spent a summer of after-work hours the year I graduated from college. Nearly every afternoon that summer, three of us would load into a car and leave the golf course, where we were the entire maintenance crew, for the drive over dirt roads to our salvation. The falls were far—they came after the sun-drenched fields, after the farthest farm, and now, to me, existed even beyond the reach of time.

There were two large pools, each as round as a clock face, bored into the granite bedrock into globes the size of hot air balloons. The top one was the best for swimming and had a wooden ladder down into it, which we used only to climb out. Water spilled from this one down the granite face into the second one, where the spout pounded in a roar. At the bottom were two smaller pools where wild trout darted from side to side, seeking shelter.

A number of people had been killed at the falls, and it was easy to see how it could happen. The risk was part of the attraction, and it only sweetened the freedom of the first leap into the upper pool. The water flowed from a brook above into a smooth halfpipe snaking down the rock wall and plunging into the upper pool. You could ride this slide, but only with tough cut–off blue jeans, and we often did. There was a shelf in the wall above it, the round–walled shelf of a former chute, risen by geologic time, where you could lie in the sun, lulled by the white sound of the plunging water.

The bottom of the upper pool sloped from shallower into deeper water. It was covered with rounded stones, the creators, along with the stronger current of former ages, of this spherical pool. You could see the stones distinctly through 12 feet of clear liquid light. A favorite trick of ours was to swim to the bottom and lift a stone heavy enough to anchor you on the floor and then, still holding your breath but with your eyes open, walk down into the deep side, testing how far you could go.

The approach to the falls was a relief in that so little had changed. The road had been paved for more of its length, but the final three miles after the turnoff at the pond were still dirt. Driving in filled me with the same sense of distance I'd had some 30 years ago, the sense of time standing still. There weren't even any new houses. We passed the few where friends from those days had lived, each invoking a raft of memories. I recognized some names on mailboxes. My wife had friends from even earlier, when she'd spent high school summers here, so between us the vacant dirt roads were alive with phantoms.

Beyond the pond, we wound down to the farm tucked in a valley that seemed made for it. Views of fields and rising forested mountains stretched in all directions, uninterrupted by power lines, other roads, or houses. We rounded the final right–angle turn, parked by the old sawmill, and changed into our suits. But there was something new.

A large sign, courtesy of the Vermont Department of Parks

and Recreation, described the dangerous falls, cited the number of deaths that had occurred there, and finished with the sentence "Swimming is not permitted." The owners of the falls and the land around them had gotten tired of being sued by accident victims and had deeded the site to the state, which had closed the falls. Was that any surprise?

We were standing there in our swimsuits, and although I looked longingly at the pool, with its seductive slide glistening in the sun, I couldn't very well ignore the sign. Such modeling comes back to haunt the irresponsible parent, right? So, clutching at roots and tree limbs, we headed for the bottom, where we might take a quick dip in the two small, tame pools. Another change caught up with us there.

Families were gathered by the pools, something we would never have seen 30 years ago. They were parents with young children, who had hiked up on a new trail from a campground a couple of miles downstream. They weren't swimming. A few teenagers were taking turns dipping in the pools, and the hikers were watching them. There was a distinct feeling of exhibit and audience about the scene, which seemed to intensify when my wife and I stepped into a pool. It was cold enough to keep you swimming and clear enough to easily see underwater. Our sons jumped in, gasping with the chill, then got out quickly, and we all clambered up a large, sun–baked rock on the shore, where we warmed up.

My wife and sons led when we scrambled back up to the top pool. On the way up I started sweating, which made me think of swimming again. But there was the not insignificant matter of the sign and my sons. So when I got up top, I was glad to see my wife and younger son already in the first pool and grinning up at us. My older son was gazing down at them and pondering either the climb down the ladder or the first big stride. I knew what I was going to do but didn't want to appear too anxious. In front of your teenage son, it's important to be cool. So when it seemed to be, I took my moment.

The step into nothingness off the edge of the top pool, into the clarity of the kettle hole 12 feet below, is liberating in its focus. There's nothing between your hurtling body and the round stones on the bottom except the windowpane of the surface, and when you plunge through it you see a little bit through yourself too. I got one of those rare, clear glimpses of myself in the past and myself now from inside the body that had been both.

For one playful moment, I transcended the wheel of time itself.

Swing Easy

We're all looking for affirmation of how we are doing, and I suspect this is one reason we play sports. Within their narrow purview, they give us immediate and easy to read feedback to this question.

I was playing golf with my son, Kelsey, on Sunday, taking shots from end to end on the lawn. The feedback I was getting from my golf club was not positive. I was chopping at the ball, twisting my wrists and contorting my torso in all sorts of ways in order to steer the ball toward the target, the coffee can buried in the far end of the lawn.

"Swing easy, Dad."

"Yeah, okay." And with a deep sigh and a release of conscious attempt to control the club and my body, I addressed the ball and swung. It worked. As my old friend, Larry, said, "Sit into the ball. Let the club do the work." And swing easy. Always easy. Like so much else, swinging a golf club is a matter of faith and of staying out of the way. Out of your own way. Just let it happen. When I try too hard, I strangle the club and my own energy. So I swung easy and trusted the club, my swing, and my inner sense of direction. The shot is in you. You just have to let it out.

And it worked. Without effort, the club head snicked the ball and carried it toward the target. Not just once, but time after time. Follow through. Let the club head momentum travel its path and pick up the ball on the way. It's almost as though you pretend the ball's not there.

"Okay Kelsey. So it works off the tee with an iron, but what about those pesky short shots, within, say, 30 yards of the green? How not to swing too much?" I asked.

He replied, "Take the club back half as much or less, and let the club head carry the ball."

So I choked up on the shaft, sat into the ball, consciously took the club back a half swing, and trusted the club head to do its job. And guess what? It did.

Again, keep yourself out of the way. Swing evenly, with both hands. Repeat, and it works again. Sit into the ball, shorten your back swing, but complete the follow through. Snick. Snick. Snick.

We begin short–game target practice. Line up three balls, go for the hole, or, coming back, the daffodils. Swing easy. Keep the ball long on the club face. Stay out of the way. Snick. Snick. Snick. I'm reminded of just how much I learn from Kelsey. Golf is just the most recent example.

We go back to hitting long again. Coming back, from the river, I swing easy, make good contact, but the ball fades right as it clears the treetops and seems to land on the asphalt, except that we don't hear any thwack or see a bounce. We look everywhere in the mowed lawn, exactly where we've been landing our tee shots all afternoon. But nothing. After a considerable search, I give up and play another ball. It's annoying when you've been playing well with one ball and then you lose it in plain sight after a decent shot. We play another half dozen holes.

As we are about to quit, I spy my ball, sitting right behind a football that's been on the lawn all along. And I realize this is yet another lesson from Kelsey: sometimes you launch something into the world—a thought, a song, a poem, a favor—and you lose it without finding out how it landed, how it was taken or received. So you look and look and eventually give up. But then suddenly you find it, right where you thought it was. It was there all along and you've changed enough to see it. And you're reminded.

Have faith. Swing easy.

Guessing the Gears on Kettle Creek

December 2012

It was an ideal place to learn how to drive a stick shift. The road was flat and straight with plenty of places to pull off. And even though my sister, Tamsen, was older than me by three years and had been driving for that much longer, she hadn't learned to drive a stick shift. But she'd just gone out and bought a used car that had one.

I liked that about Tamsen. She had a soft spot for the car. Maybe it was cheap or spiffy or she liked the color, but for whatever reason she didn't let the fact that she couldn't drive it stop her from buying it.

You could say her decision was impetuous or naive or even presumptuous. But I think of it as showing a certain confidence in her ability to figure things out and even master them. She just liked the car, and didn't give much thought to its transmission, or her lack of experience with it.

"That's no big deal, right?" she said.

The car she bought was a sporty, white, hard-top Corvair, with a completely red interior: seats, carpet, even the dashboard, everything except the shift knob, which was white. The stick shift rose from the flat floor between the two front bucket seats. One of the neatest things about the car was that it had a four-speed transmission, the racy one, not just the standard three–speed. This might even have been why Tamsen bought it.

It was a hot summer day, the kind where you can smell the oil beginning to soften on the road. We both got in, with me driving, and headed down the long straightaway on Kettle Creek Road. As I shifted, I explained to Tamsen the need to coordinate the timing when you pushed in the clutch and when you moved the stick into the next gear.

"See, like this," I said, while demonstrating in slow motion. "When the engine sounds like it's peaked, push the clutch in, and move the stick from one gear to another."

"You've also got to take your foot off the gas when you shift. If you don't, this is what happens." The whining engine screamed, and I shouted above it, "AND YOU'LL HAVE TO YELL, LIKE THIS!" We both started laughing.

I drove the length of the straightaway, carefully repeating the demonstration and taking pains to do everything in slow motion. Then I pulled into a driveway, turned the car around, and switched seats with Tamsen.

She pressed on the gas pedal and the clutch, put the stick in first gear, and let the clutch out all at once.

The car stalled right away.

She chuckled, looked at me, and said, "What happened?"

"I forgot to show you how to let the clutch out gently while slowly depressing the gas pedal," I said. "Sorry about that. So this time let the clutch out slowly as you feel it engage. First gear's the trickiest. You'll get it."

She started the car, looked at the dashboard, and said, "Okay. Let the clutch out slowly and at the same time give it gas slightly."

"Right," I said.

She stalled again.

"That was better. You're relaxing a bit," I said, encouragingly.

She took a deep breath and said, "Okay, I'm getting the feel of the clutch. This time I've got it. No problem."

She started the car, carefully moved the stick into first, and while gradually pressing the gas pedal, slowly let the clutch out. When it was finally moving, but just barely, she let the clutch out all the way, all of a sudden, and we launched like a rocket, now looking through the windshield at the beautiful summer clouds overhead.

Tamsen's natural response was to let up on the gas pedal, which, thankfully, brought the front wheels back down to the road. But immediately sensing the engine was about to stall, she'd stand on the accelerator, which brought us roaring back to life and sent the front wheels skyward once more. This continued until, with my head shaking so rapidly that my sight was blurred, I yelled, "STEP ON THE CLUTCH!" whereupon we coasted to the side of the road, with the engine wheezing in little puffs. Tamsen was laughing uproariously. Her cheeks were rosy, her eyes wide open. I was scratching my head.

"That was quite a ride, don't you think?" she said chuckling.

After we both caught our breath, I explained in greater detail why the clutch had to be let out slowly while pushing down the gas pedal and, after a few more corral starts, she got the hang of it and was able to get the car moving without launching loose items on the dashboard to the floor.

But hurdles lay ahead. Once we got rolling, the engine reached enough speed to require shifting gears. And although the gear pattern was embossed on the white shift knob in an "H," she didn't follow the same sequence. Pulling the stick backward from first gear, Tamsen allowed it to drift to the right when it reached the neutral gate, and pulled it into fourth gear instead. The car lugged uncontrollably, jerking in small hops down the road as she dutifully stepped on the gas.

"What's going on? I made a smooth shift, didn't I?" she asked, smiling at me.

"Yeah, you did, just into fourth gear. We want to go into second. Try pushing in the clutch, and moving the stick straight back from first, like the 'H' on the knob," I said.

"Okay, straight back," she said, smiling. And then she did it.

"Wow, check it out," she said, laughing. "We're actually driving smoothly down the road in second gear. I'm getting this, yes sir!"

We soon learned that starting out was one thing but shifting through the gears was another. When she did shift into second and needed to find third ("up and away," I'd remind her) she pushed straight up through neutral into first gear. The engine screamed again, slowing the Corvair suddenly, and anything on the rear deck was now on the back seat.

Because of her difficulty finding the next gear, I asked Tamsen, "What gear are we in?" Then "What gear do we want to go to next?" and finally, "Where is it located? Ready? Shift!" I repeated this chorus each time I heard engine speed building, trying not to shout over the crescendo from the crankshaft.

Tamsen would shout, "Okay, next gear, yes sireee!" and boldly push the stick toward it.

Within an hour, she had smoothed the start–off and changing through the gears, and was now pretty good at shifting a four–speed transmission. The whole time, she'd laughed at her blunders, her laughter accentuated by the lurching, leaping car. I'd been serious at first, but her laughter was contagious, and by the end we were roaring together.

When we finished, her driving had smoothed considerably, and when we got out of the car, we were still laughing. As we walked toward the house together she said, "You know, that was really fun."

She'd gone from novice to proficient in one short afternoon, had been laughing all the way through it, and still was. No big deal, right?

Every Parent's Frontier

November 2013

"Hugh, you did that too easily. Try walking it backward with your eyes closed," John said. I had just walked a log between two trees that was 30 feet off the ground. John was our instructor at Outward Bound, and this exercise was one of our base camp activities. I quickly thought about what he had said at orientation, that it was challenge by choice, your prerogative to participate, that no one was going to make you. And then I tried. And succeeded.

I've thought of that Teacher's Practicum course a lot since becoming the father of two boys. The first time I thought of it occurred when I was still getting used to the nocturnal routine with infants: the middle of the night feedings, the diaper changes, the teething. I remember feeling tired all the time and how surprised I was at actually getting used to it. And then I remembered how tired, but energized too, I had been at Outward Bound, and, in particular, that first expedition with my crew. We'd been out for two days, had bushwhacked (using no trails) 30 miles and, returning about 1:00 a.m., were, by about 8 hours, the last group in. Too tired to look back, people up front asked whoever it was in the back with the lit flashlight to turn it off. It took us a little while to realize that there was no lit flashlight, that what they had seen were fireflies.

"I've never hallucinated before," someone said.

"Guess we're pretty tired," another voice replied.

I thought of that night ten years later when our son Graham got croup. After a number of phone consultations, our doctor requested that we bring him to the hospital. It was 2:00 a.m. His cough had begun to sound alien, to the point where it was frightening him to tears, and my wife and I were quaking. I comforted Graham in the hospital oxygen tent, where we clung to each other in a clammy mist until daylight, when his breathing had eased. Relieved, I drove straight to my first–period class at the high school, where I taught English.

But physical challenges weren't the only, or the most important, at Outward Bound, and neither are they with fatherhood. The emotional tests probe your strength in other ways.

The instant you fall while rock climbing your anxiety soars as, just before the rope comes taut, you wonder whether the protection will pull out. That same tension causes the lump in your throat as you watch your three–year–old approach a peer group new to him and hope with all faith that the experience won't be painful for him, or for you. The test of faith, of course, is that if you've done it right, both the rope and your son's confidence will hold up and you can smile.

Unlike Outward Bound, though, where instructors were always present, there is no blueprint for parenting, or, if there is, it's revealed to you later. So I make up the plan as I go, letting my love for my sons and my incomplete knowledge of the world be my guide. The plan has some erasure marks on it, but it's still legible. It helps a lot that my wife and I share the same blueprint most of the time.

Parenting also differs from Outward Bound in that there are

no definite endings. Outward Bound lasted only 23 days. When I hopped on the bus at Outward Bound for the airport, my Teacher's Practicum was over. We took what we had gained and went home inspired. As a parent for my children, I will always be "home" for them. They'll become teenagers, then adults, then parents themselves, but they are always your children even while, during that time, you've changed too.

In both arenas the rewards are present as well as the challenges. Our final individual exam at Outward Bound was a 13-mile run on the last day, an event that, like your child's graduation, you've known all along has been coming. With 90 other chilled runners under a predawn moon, you half listen as the instructor briefly outlines the route over the mountains, across the fields, down the dry creekbeds and jeep trails, a route you know ends with a lung-burning two-mile hill. And you wonder: can I do this thing, which is not easy, which I've never done before? And then you start.

Along the way, over the course of nearly two hours of running, you're conscious of losing the night and gaining the day. With five miles left, a race marshal hoots you on, telling you that it's all downhill from here. Except, of course, for those last two miles. When you cross the finish line you've completed a search as much as you have a race. And what you've found inside yourself is buried treasure.

With parenting, the rewards are not always so structured; they tend to arrive in a more spontaneous fashion. As when my three-year-old approaches a friend of mine, says hello and asks them how they are. Or when I stumble upon him reading *The Lorax* out loud to himself and I listen secretly behind a door, sneaking peeks. Or even when, out of the blue, he says, "Daddy, I love you." Or what may be even more of a compliment: "Daddy, you're fun to play with."

It seems we're always going out into the world in some way, and the challenges are always there, and so are the choices.

Take your pick.

Spring Migration

May 2015

The whole planet is tilting with a momentum you can see all around. Now, at just about the halfway point between the vernal equinox and the summer solstice, the Northern hemisphere bows toward the sun and triggers the global migrations. As the sunlight increases in the north, so does all life. The herds of caribou, vast flocks of songbirds, and pods of whales journey by land, air, and ocean to their summer breeding grounds, driven by the lengthening daylight and the bountiful food. And many families of man also move toward the sunlight, following their herds to fresh pasturage. Having endured the long winter of hauling hay and water to their animals, nomadic herdsmen in Mongolia and the farmers in the Swiss Alps move to high ground, where they find a renewal of energy. Some humans, seeking not sustenance or breeding grounds, travel for spiritual rejuvenation to places they consider holy. Pilgrims in Tibet circle the entire 32–mile base of Mt. Kailash, the source of some of the longest rivers in Asia. Some make the journey on their knees, reaffirming connection with their Buddhist gods.

And so it is that every spring our family performs its own renewal ritual. We too travel north; the destination is also a mountain; the element we seek is that which sustains all life:

water. Water frozen by the long winter and high altitude of Mt. Washington, in New Hampshire, becomes the highest source of snow in the east of North America.

Our family has made this journey for over 40 years, joining many others over that time. The pilgrimage for all is arduous. In the parking lot, we read license plates from Colorado and Florida, Quebec and California. We pack our skis, boots, poles, food, and clothing for the two hours up the steep snow–and–mud trail to Tuckerman's Ravine. There we drop our packs and shoulder our skis and poles up the headwall to our launching sites. Frequently, the weather can be miserable. We've climbed through snow, hail, rain, and fog with May temperatures in the twenties and winds strong enough to drive the precipitation horizontal.

Due to conflicting schedules, we usually can't pick optimal conditions. Some years we've arrived early, and the headwall is frozen, unclimbable and unskiable. Other years we're late, and the snowfield has shrunk or the avalanche danger is high. And although skiing is the central activity, not all of us come to ski, but still choose to cope with whatever conditions we find. Our aim is to complete the journey however we can. The goal may be simple, then, but even under the best conditions the trip is challenging.

The reasons for making it are as varied and complex as the conditions can be. For skiers, Tuckerman's Ravine is a proving ground. The 56–degree slope presents a formidable level of physical and psychological challenge. On a sunny day, the tone in the Ravine is light, with crowds of spectators gathered on the floor of the bowl, watching those descending. The fans are observant, erupting into choruses of concern with one skier's dramatic fall, echoes of laughter with another's humorous display, or cheers and whistles at a particularly sterling and ambitious descent.

But the minds of the skiers are packed with full–bore focus.

To climb the headwall is to ascend a steep ladder in ski boots, holding skis on your shoulders with one hand and poles in the other hand. Looking down over the rim, the slope is so steep it disappears from view. When the slope comes back into view below, the skiers are tiny. And because skiers tap their reserves when hiking, carrying, and climbing, often there's only enough energy for one run or, regarding the pitch, one fall, whichever comes first. These pilgrims come to answer a question we all ask ourselves at some point: Just how deep are my reserves?

Hardships endured together bring people closer. Crew rowing and team triathlons produce such a bond: that it's rewarding to push yourself beyond your normal limits; that a shared experience of giving your all boosts mutual respect. Over beer at the end of the day, you rest affirmed, not only because you met a challenge but also because you did it together. The memories of these shared experiences are everlasting.

Beyond kinship and challenge, though, we go for reasons that are deeper. The water and rock cycles are dominant features among the peaks; here nature speaks boldly. The alpine scale dwarfs us and commandingly turns us to the raw forces that have shaped our history as well as the places of our origin. Like the whales, caribou, and birds, we come back with the sun to find renewal. We speak, as all pilgrims do, with our bodies and our journeys, to confirm our sense of place as a part of the earth. And in so doing, we say we are mountain people, that our identities lie among the peaks where the rivers begin and that we need to return to them lest we forget who we are.

Provence

July 2017

At first, it was the sounds of the birds in the night, in the palm tree fronds we could touch from our beds outdoors on the second floor deck, birds that we later realized had to be tree frogs, playing background for the music festival in the distance, pounding into the early morning.

Then it became the wandering streets of Arles, strewn with the confetti of art shows, galleries, outdoor expositions, and restaurants. The heat led us back to the town square and its welcoming ice cream and shade.

With the Renault, a/c in full service, we looped the rotaries, launched from their scribed arcs by our Google–linked driver and navigator across the plains of orchards and cropland, with their windbreaks of fence–straight poplar and cypress, toward Le Pont du Gard. Upon our arrival, the billowing sycamores spread their canopies, ushering the heat to open ground.

The towering arcs of the aqueduct invoked the spirits of Roman slaves 20 centuries gone, crawling scaffolding 16 stories into the sky. The air hung with the echoed, clanking strains of their labor. We leapt from the river's ledges into the clear, blue–green water, and hobbled across the stony beach to the relief of shade. At night we climbed into our beds on the second–floor deck, where the wind swirled the palm fronds aside our heads and swept our dreams into the heavens.

Then it became the hallway-narrow road across the rice paddy-flat expanses of Le Camargue, when oncoming traffic passed with pulse-spiking nearness at speeds that raised from us shrieks of nervous laughter. Brigades of white flamingos lined the distant shores of the salt basins, like mirages shimmering in the heat.

On the beach at Piemanson, the swallows swooped the cresting waves in wind that rushed and swept them from view. We played bocce and hunted one another under water, our playful attacks yielding gleeful shouts of false surprise. Shells of azure angel wings sprinkled the sand.

With an early start, we threaded the traffic and tunnels of Marseille without misstep, drawn by the remote, brilliant turquoise of secluded coves, Les Calanques, exactly to the trailhead. The ever-present wind had closed them—fire danger. We retraced our route, quiet with our dashed anticipation, and found a new beach near home, grateful for the waves under the warm sun and the luscious slices of melon the woman at the fruit stand offered us.

Then came a day of hilltop villages. We walked the cobbled streets of Lacoste, wandering up past artists working in their studios, with window boxes spilling bands of color, to a view of olive orchards and fields of sunflowers and lavender stretching to the horizon of rolling hills. In Bonnieux, we climbed narrow alleys under ship-mast pines and archways to a medieval church and a long view back to Lacoste and, again, the distant diamonds of olives, lavender, sunflowers, and poppies.

Drawn to the cinnamon cliffs of Roussillon, we climbed its spiral main street past vermillion galleries, scarlet shops, and ruby restaurants to its top, where we found an artist whose work we wanted to take home. Four small, stacked watercolors bloomed off the paper with fields of poppy, sunflower, lavender, and olive.

In Les Baux, at the Carrières de Luminières, we marveled at the colossal images towering above us by Bosch, Brueghel, and Arcimboldo, cast by one hundred projectors onto the floor and walls of the quarry inside the mountain.

On our last day, hurrying to return the Renault, we got lost in the labyrinth of Arles's narrow, inner streets but still managed to make the deadline. Four weary travelers rode the long train ride to Zurich, where, late at night, we found our way, with two trams and a bus ride in a network under construction, to Gockhausen, where a sleepy coyote emerged from the bushes. Exhausted, we stumbled to the inn, where we slept the sleep of those too long awake, France now behind us in time but with us always in our hearts.

Acknowledgements

I began writing these essays over twenty years ago during small windows of time, only sharing them with family and a few friends, whose support enabled me to continue. This is how I incurred my first round of debts. I wish to thank especially George Erb, Doris Kuller, Laurent Benedetti, Tom Fahsbender, Larry Herrick, Roger Behrens, Faye Gage, Ann Croley, Donald Gallo, Mary Sullivan, and Margaret Miner. If not for them, I know these essays would be a row of file folders on my shelf.

My brother Ben provided key information for the essay on our Mt. Shasta climb. He also tied flies for our brother, Tim, and me. I am thankful to both for their support.

I am indebted to June Fiorelli, a friend who knew my parents since she and they were all young. With this knowledge of my family's generations as well as her own experience writing and publishing, she has compassionately guided my aspirations and my writing.

I want to thank David Dvorkin, who designed and formatted the interior of the book, as well as its cover. His patience with my many questions and his full belief in helping writers produce professional quality books kept me from wandering alone in the world of digital publishing.

For her help with software glitches I thank Jessica Zaccagnini, who's timely, first rate help saved me from technical disasters and their depths of despair.

All I've published has benefitted from the suggestions and professional editing of Suzi Arensberg Diacou. Her skill, experience and detailed attention have taught me a great deal and I listen to her carefully.

I am grateful to our sons, Kelsey and Graham, first of all for their support all along. But I also know that, having lost my father when I was 3, I've always wondered what kind of person he was, or thought he was, or hoped he was, and I hope that these essays have served the purpose of helping them see that about their father.

My greatest debt is to my wife. For over forty-two years she has provided steadfast encouragement and a keen sense of balance in the adventures we share. She is the bedrock of my foundation.

About the Author

After a 30-year career teaching English, writing, and outdoor education, Hugh Rogers lives with his wife, Monique, and their cat, Bagheera, in the Northwest Hills of Connecticut.

www.ingramcontent.com/pod-product-compliance
Lightning Source LLC
Chambersburg PA
CBHW050113280326
41933CB00010B/1084